THE DARBYS

OF

COALBROOKDALE

By the same author:

A Victorian MP and his Constituents (1966)
The Industrial Revolution in Shropshire (1973, new edition 1981)
'The Most Extraordinary District in the World': Ironbridge and Coalbrookdale (1977, new edition 1988)
The Iron Bridge: Symbol of the Industrial Revolution (with Neil Cossons, 1979)
Yeomen and Colliers in Telford: the probate inventories of Dawley, Lilleshall, Wellington and Wrockwardine (with Jeff Cox, 1980)
Victorian Banbury (1982)
The Making of the Industrial Landscape (1982)
A History of Shropshire (1983)
Victorian Shrewsbury (1984)
The Blackwell Encyclopaedia of Industrial Archaeology (1992)

THE DARBYS
OF
COALBROOKDALE

BARRIE TRINDER

Published in association with
Ironbridge Gorge Museum Trust
by

PHILLIMORE

First published 1974
Revised reprint 1978
Revised and corrected reprint 1981
Japanese edition, Shinhyoron, Tokyo, 1986

This entirely new edition published 1991 by
PHILLIMORE & CO. LTD.,
Shopwyke Hall,
Chichester, Sussex, PO20 6BQ

ISBN 0 85033 791 7

Printed and bound in Great Britain by
BIDDLES LTD
Guildford and King's Lynn

CONTENTS

Foreword ix

1   The Setting 1

2   The First Generation 3

3   The Transformation of the Iron Industry 15

4   Coalbrookdale at its Zenith 25

5   The War-Time Years 41

6   Depression and Recovery 47

7   Homes and Families 59

8   Survivals 66

Further Reading 71

Index 73

PLATES

1 A view of the Upper Works at Coalbrookdale 2
2 The works yard, Coalbrookdale, *c*.1880 7
3 The forehearth of the Old Furnace, Coalbrookdale 11
4 Dale House, Coalbrookdale 12
5 The Old Row, Horsehay 21
6 Sunniside, 1750 23
7 An Afternoon View of Coalbrookdale, by William
   Williams 30
8 The Iron Bridge 34
9 A bridge across the Kennet and Avon canal 42
10 A whaling pot 45
11 The Wellington or Halfpenny Bridge 49
12 The Macclesfield Bridge 50
13 Abraham Darby IV 51
14 Cast-iron statue of Oliver Cromwell 53
15 Steam engine built by the Coalbrookdale Company 56
16 The second Sunniside 60
17 Rosehill House 62
18 The study, Rosehill House 67
19 The dining room, Rosehill House 68
20 The Old Furnace, Coalbrookdale 69

FIGURES

1. The Darby family tree 26

2. The Shropshire ironworks of the Derby-
    Reynolds-Rathbone partnerships, *c.*1790 29

3. Shropshire ironworks owned by the Darby
    family in the 19th century 48

4. Sketch map of Coalbrookdale 61

FOREWORD

This book was first published in 1974 to fulfil the demand for a straightforward but accurate and up-to-date account of the role of the Darby family in the industrial history of Shropshire. The popularity of the Ironbridge Gorge with tourists and with educational groups attests to the continuing need for such a publication, and a new edition provides an opportunity for including some of the findings of more recent research, particularly the work of Nancy Cox on Abraham Darby I and of Lady Labouchere on Abiah Darby. I am grateful to John Powell, Librarian to the Ironbridge Gorge Museum, for bringing to my attention numerous other sources and references. Most of the material used here is to be found, though differently treated, in my *Industrial Revolution in Shropshire* (second edition, Phillimore, 1981), which is fully referenced. Sources published since 1981 are listed in the bibliography.

I am grateful, as ever, to all who have aided my researches into Shropshire history, and to those who have contributed photographs for this volume.

February 1992   BARRIE TRINDER

Chapter 1

THE SETTING

THE IRON BRIDGE in Shropshᵢ   Britain's most celebrated industrial monument. Every year hundreds of thousands of people from all parts of the world visit the bridge. It is the most dramatic reminder of a time two centuries ago when the coal-field in which the bridge stands was the foremost iron-making area in the world, when innovations were developed in this part of Shropshire which have shaped much of the world in which we live. While most of the landscape of the district has changed, the bridge stands as a spectacular memorial to the skills of the most imaginative generation of Shropshire ironmasters.

Many of those who visit the Iron Bridge also make their way to Coalbrookdale, the ironworking village about a mile to the west, where the ribs for the bridge were cast. There, in the Museum of Iron, it is possible to examine the products of the foundry which has been working in the valley for over three centuries, as well as the blast furnace where iron ore was first successfully smelted with coke instead of charcoal. Coal-brookdale retains many of the houses and public buildings erected in the 18th and 19th centuries. On the hillside above the village is the graveyard of the local Quaker meeting. The meeting house to which it was appended has been demolished and the gravestones have been moved from their original positions to stand around the high boundary wall. Visitors who make their way to the graveyard notice that the simple, unostentatious stone memorials commemorate a relatively small number of families. There are Gilpins, who served for several generations as clerks in the ironworks, and Luccocks, the first of whom was apprenticed at Coalbrookdale in 1714. There are Edges, black-smiths who came to Shropshire from Norfolk in the 1790s and developed the use of wrought-iron chains for winding coal

Plate 1. A view of the Upper Works at Coalbrookdale, by George Perry and T. Vivares, c.1758. On the left is the old blast furnace with its surrounding foundry buildings. An engine cylinder is being hauled by the team of horses in the left foreground, while on the edge of the furnace pool coal is being coked in open heaps. In the background can be seen the mixture of ironmasters' houses and workers' cottages which characterised Coalbrookdale.

mines. There is a stone marking the grave of William Reynolds, the most enlightened and most intellectually able of the Shropshire iron-masters. Above all there are memorials to generations of the Darby family, with whom the history of Coalbrookdale is inextricably linked.

Every history book which discusses the iron industry in the 18th century mentions 'Abraham Darby' of Coalbrookdale. In some accounts the impression is given that this 'Abraham Darby' combined the innovative versatility of Leonardo da Vinci with the longevity of Methuselah, and was making inventions at Coalbrookdale from the dawn of the 18th century until the Great Exhibition of 1851. Confusion was compounded in 1981 when British Rail conferred the name 'Abraham Darby' on locomotive 86 247. There were four men called Abraham Darby who managed the Coalbrookdale ironworks, together, in later generations, with other works of the Coalbrookdale Company, and other members of the family with different forenames were also concerned with the direction of the works.

Chapter 2

THE FIRST GENERATION

THE DARBYS of Coalbrookdale were descended from John Darby, a locksmith who lived at Old Farm Lodge by the hill called the Wren's Nest near Dudley in the Black Country. John Darby's father, also called John, had lived in the same house. John Darby spent the last years of his life at the Lodge, Madeley, the home of his daughter, Esther, and son-in-law, where he died in 1725. John Darby was a member of the Society of Friends, nicknamed the Quakers, then a new religious group, having been founded in the 1650s. Like many peasant craftsmen, John Darby probably found the tenets of the sect closely relevant to his situation, and Quakerism was to determine the pattern of life of subsequent generations of his family.

John Darby's son, known to history as Abraham Darby I, was born on 14 April 1678. Nothing is known of his early life, but in the early 1690s he was apprenticed to another Quaker, Jonathan Freeth, maker of malt mills in Birmingham. Malt mills were about the size of the large types of 20th-century food mixers. Their steel blades broke up grains of malt prior to its use in brewing. When his apprenticeship was concluded in 1699, Abraham Darby married Mary Sargeant, and moved to Bristol, a city where Quakers were becoming prominent in the business community. He first made his living as a maker of malt mills, perhaps the first in the city, but in 1702 he became a partner with other Quakers in a brass works at Baptist Mills, of which he appears to have been the manager.

The manufacture of brass, an alloy of copper and zinc, was expanding in Britain generally, and in Bristol in particular at this time. Darby seems to have been responsible for introducing the use of coal rather than charcoal in brass-making furnaces, and for bringing to Bristol workers from the continent, skilled in manufacturing and fabricating brass. In 1703 he started a new enterprise, a foundry for casting iron pots, in Cheese Lane, Bristol, and four years later took out a patent for casting such pots in sand, a technology which had been used by brass-founders for making taps and small cooking pots. Pig-iron for the foundry was purchased from the blast furnaces at Blakeney and Redbrook in the Forest of Dean.

Abraham Darby gradually developed links with Coalbrookdale, in the Severn Gorge in Shropshire. He may have known something of the locality from the time of his apprenticeship, since steel of the kind used for the blades of malt mills was made at Coalbrookdale. Darby was involved with a brass works in Coalbrookdale which had probably been in operation since the 1690s, and in 1706 he was a witness to the purchase of land for the Quaker burial ground at Broseley on the south bank of the Severn in the Gorge.

Just as Darby had interests in Bristol in working both brass and iron, so his concern with the brass trade in Shropshire was followed by involvement in iron-making.

The iron industry operated on a regional basis. The West Midlands and Borderland region was united by the Severn navigation, and linked by coastal shipping and sometimes by overland carriage with works and mines in South Wales, Cheshire, Lancashire and the Lake District. Within the region were many remote ironworks, which constantly exchanged iron at different stages of production. The greatest demand was for wrought-iron, in the form of rods or bars, which could be forged and hammered by craftsmen into nails, tools, chains, locks and other items for domestic and commercial use. The greatest concentration of smiths making such products was in Darby's native Black Country, and much of the wrought-iron made in the region was distributed to them from fairs at Dudley and Stourbridge.

Wrought-iron is a commercially pure form of iron, in which a small proportion of slag is physically mixed, giving it a fibrous form. It can be shaped when it is heated by being hammered or passed through rollers, and was an ideal material for use by craftsmen who had little power at their disposal other than that of their own strong arms. By about 1700 wrought-iron was always manufactured in Britain by a two-stage process. Iron ore was heated in a blast furnace, a substantial masonry structure, with a fuel (usually charcoal) and a flux (usually limestone). The furnace would be blown by bellows operated by a water wheel, and normally worked continuously for six to eight months of the year, stopping only in the summer months when water supplies were insufficient to work the bellows. As the bellows raised the temperature in the furnace, droplets of iron would trickle down to the crucible, the lower part of the structure. The limestone would also melt and, because it was less dense than the molten iron, floated above it, fusing many of the impurities present in the ore and the fuel. Twice a day the furnace would be tapped. First the slag was drawn off, to solidify, and to be discarded as waste. Then the iron would be allowed to run out, usually into a channel made in sand, with closed-off channels branching off at right angles from it. The iron in these channels was thought to resemble piglets feeding from a sow, hence for generations before 1700 it had been known as pig-iron.

The product of the blast furnace was cast-iron, a form of iron with a carbon content of about four per cent. In the 16th century English ironworkers had known that it was possible to make useful and even beautiful objects by pouring cast-iron into moulds and allowing it to solidify, but in reality by 1700 comparatively little iron was used as cast-iron. Most of the pigs made at blast furnaces were taken to other works called forges where they were converted to wrought-iron.

At a forge the pig-iron was first heated in a small, beehive-shaped hearth called a finery, fired with charcoal, and blown by a blast of air from a water-powered bellows. The iron would melt, and the operator, the finer, would stir it with a bar. The oxygen in the air would unite with the carbon in the iron and after some time the pig-iron would be converted to a crude form of wrought-iron. From the finery the iron would be taken to a water-powered hammer which would shape it into a regular block called a bloom, at the same time expelling many impurities. At the next stage the iron would be reheated in a furnace rather like the finery but without the air blast, which was called a chafery. When it reached a sufficient temperature it was returned to the hammer and shaped into a form suitable for the next stage of manufacture. Most craftsmen required iron in sections thinner than could be made with a powerful but rather clumsy hammer, and much of the iron from forges was taken to slitting mills. At a rolling mill the rough bars which emerged from hammers were first flattened into long strips between plain cylindrical rollers powered by water wheels. The strip was then passed between rotating discs which cut it into bars suitable for use by nailmakers and other craftsmen.

The blast furnaces of the West Midlands and the Borderland were situated near to the sources of iron ore, mostly around the edges of the coalfields, on streams which provided power for their bellows. From the blast furnaces pig-iron was distributed to different forges, since ironmasters knew that they could produce particular qualities in their wrought-iron by mixing proportions of pig-iron from different areas. Forges in north Shropshire drew their pig-iron not just from the nearby furnaces around the Severn Gorge, but from the Clee Hills, the Forest of Dean, from Lancashire, Cheshire, and even the American colonies. The greatest concentration of forges was to be found in the valley of the Worcestershire Stour. In Shropshire clusters of forges were located in the valleys of the River Tern and its tributaries, on the south slopes of the Clee Hills, and in the area immediately south of Shrewsbury. Like furnaces, forges needed water to power their bellows, and charcoal for use as fuel, so they were always situated on streams, and in areas where reasonable supplies of charcoal could be obtained.

The supply of charcoal was the most severe of the constraints which inhibited the growth of the British iron industry. Charcoal was made from cord wood, from trees of about twenty years' growth, specially raised as a crop in coppices. Supplies could be increased in the long term only by the large-scale coppicing of land previously used for other purposes. In the short term, to increase the consumption of charcoal in one year caused a shortage in subsequent years. Ironmasters competed for supplies. Many people in the 17th century attempted to

smelt iron ore using coal instead of charcoal, the most celebrated of them being the Black Countryman Dud Dudley, but
none had succeeded in making iron of a satisfactory quality.

The area to which Abraham Darby moved in the first
decade of the 18th century was already busily involved in
mining and manufacturing. Coalbrookdale lies at the western
end of the Severn Gorge where the river cuts through the hills
of the Shropshire coalfield. Mines, supplying coal which was
traded along the River Severn, had been operating on a
considerable scale since the 16th century while coal was used
locally for brick-making, lime-burning, firing clay tobacco pipes,
and making glass, amongst other purposes. By 1700 the Gorge,
for nearly a century, had been one of the two nurseries of the
English railway. The longwall system of extracting coal had
been employed there for 50 years or more, and was called the
Shropshire method. The Severn itself was one of the busiest
commercial waterways in Europe.

The district was already of some importance in the iron
trade. Four blast furnaces, at Coalbrookdale, Willey, Kemberton
and Leighton, were situated around the edges of the coalfield.
Forest of Dean pig-iron, and pig-iron from the American
colonies, passed through the Severn Gorge en route to the

Plate 2. The works yard, Coalbrookdale, *c.*1880. While the railway
wagons and street lamps show this to be a 19th-century picture, much of
the atmosphere of the foundry, the mixture of untidy buildings, sand,
patterns and finished castings, would have been much the same in the
early 18th century.

forges of north Shropshire and mid-Wales, and wrought-iron from these forges passed downstream to the slitting mills and iron-working craftsmen of south Staffordshire and north Worcestershire.

The name 'Coalbrookdale' was sometimes applied to the whole of the Severn Gorge, but strictly speaking it should be used only of the steep-sided tributary valley in Madeley parish on the north bank of the Severn at the western end of the Gorge, which extends from the river to the confluence of two streams about a mile to the north. At the time of the dissolution of the monasteries in the 1530s the monks of Wenlock Priory had a bloomery in Coalbrookdale. This was an ancient form of iron furnace, making wrought-iron in small quantities by a direct method, which was superseded as the blast furnace and its associated forge spread through England in the 16th century. In the early 17th century Coalbrookdale was the scene of important innovations by Sir Basil Brooke, lord of the manor of Madeley. Before 1642 Brooke was working a steel works in Coalbrookdale. At this time steel, an alloy of iron and carbon, containing no more than 1.7 per cent carbon and used for weapons and tools, was made only in small quantities. Brooke's probably employed a new method of steel-making which he had introduced to England about 1620.

It is uncertain when the first blast furnace was built at Coalbrookdale. The date on the beam of the present Old Furnace now appears to be 1638, but before the furnace was uncovered in the 1950s it was usually taken to be 1658. Old photographs also suggest that the third figure in the date was a '5'. Documentary evidence is inconclusive, but tends to suggest that no blast furnace had been built before the outbreak of the Civil War in 1642. There was certainly a blast furnace at Coalbrookdale by 1660, and it was to be the centre of industrial activities there for a further century and a half.

In the latter part of the 17th century the Coalbrookdale iron-works does not seem to have been particularly prosperous. Those who worked it did not belong to any of the large partnerships which dominated the iron trade in the region, and they seem to have had difficulties in obtaining supplies of charcoal in a competitive market. The last-known person to work it before the arrival of Abraham Darby was a certain Shadrach Fox. During a flood, probably between 1700 and 1706, water entered the blast furnace and there was an explosion which rendered it a ruin. Fox ceased to work it and went to Russia in the service of Peter the Great. In 1712 his son Meshack returned from Russia and attempted, without success, to recover his father's lease of Coalbrookdale.

In 1708 Abraham Darby leased the blast furnace at Coalbrookdale, then in a derelict state. In the autumn of that year his workmen began to reconstruct it. The old hearth was knocked down, and new hearthstones, probably blocks of sandstone from Arley, were brought up the Severn. New hide bellows were made. By Christmas the work was complete and payments were being recorded for 'warming ye furnes' prior to putting it into blast.

The furnace which Darby used stood on the site of the present 'Old Blast Furnace'. Its stone foundations are probably those which are still visible. It is clear that in 1709 Abraham Darby used coke instead of charcoal as his fuel, and that while doing so he was obtaining iron of a reasonable quality. This was the first time that iron had been successfully made using a mineral fuel rather than charcoal, in spite of the many experiments which had been made in the previous century. Darby succeeded where others had failed because he used coke instead of raw coal, and because the Shropshire clod coal from which the coke was made was largely free of sulphur. Darby's knowledge of coke came from his past involvement with the malt trade. His daughter-in-law, in an account of his life, says significantly that 'he had coal coak'd into Cynder, *as is done for drying Malt*. He would also have gained some acquaintance with the use of mineral fuel in the Bristol brass trade. From the time the furnace began to operate payments were being made to workmen for 'charcking coals', and the accounts show beyond any question that these were coals dug from pits in the ground, and not charcoal.

At first Darby employed relatively few people at the furnace. John Tylor, the founder, John Felton, the keeper, Richard Hart, the filler, Richard Knowls, the stocker of the bridge, and Richard Bear, the mine (i.e. iron ore) burner, were the principal workmen. Day labourers were hired to do various unskilled tasks. All the raw materials were purchased from local mines operated by other people. Darby bought iron ore from Richard Hartshorne, one of the most prominent entrepreneurs in the coalfield, who leased extensive tracts of land for mining from several landowners. Limestone was purchased from quarries on Benthall Edge and around Much Wenlock. Some workers from Bristol were brought to Coalbrookdale. They included John Thomas, with whom Darby had made an agreement regarding the making of bellied pots, and Thomas Luccock, the first of many bearers of that name to work at Coalbrookdale. From the first Darby used iron from the furnace to make castings, which included kettles, pots and 'furnaces', as the bellied pots made under the 1707 patent were called.

After the first year or so of operation Darby experienced difficulties with the furnace. The quantities of iron castings and pig-iron taken down the Severn to Bristol fell both in 1710 and 1711, and in 1712 the operation was in such difficulty that some of Darby's partners were trying to withdraw their capital. Samuel Smiles, the 19th-century historian who was able to see an account book which has now been lost, suggests that Darby experimented with various mixtures of fuel between 1710 and 1714. Recent research, particularly that on the Port Books of Gloucester which record traffic on the River Severn, confirms that this was so. Darby bought wood to make charcoal, which appears to have been mixed with coke and charged to the furnace. He also brought both coal and coke from Bristol, and coal from Neath in South Wales. Production of castings seems to have increased substantially, and in 1715 Darby constructed a second blast furnace at Coalbrookdale. It was unusual for an ironworks to include more than one blast furnace, but water power at Coalbrookdale was abundant, and while it would have been difficult to secure sufficient charcoal to fire two furnaces, it was possible to obtain enough coking coal to satisfy the demands of many more than two. Darby also built air furnaces, reverberatory furnaces in which pig-iron was re-melted for making castings, which could be worked when the blast furnace was not operating in the summer months. By the time of Darby's death in 1717 he had established a flourishing foundry business, using improved technology to provide pots and kettles of superior quality to those previously available.

The foundry at Coalbrookdale was only a small part of the series of enterprises which Darby and his partners planned in Shropshire. They were already concerned with the brass works in Coalbrookdale before the leasing of the blast furnace in 1708. By 1710 it seems that Darby was developing a copper smelter adjacent to the blast furnace at Coalbrookdale, perhaps

Plate 3. The forehearth of the Old Furnace, Coalbrookdale. This photograph was probably taken in the 19th century when the furnace remains were incorporated within a building. It certainly predates by many years the restoration of the furnace in 1959.

because there were difficulties in obtaining copper for the brass works. In that year he signed an agreement for rights to mine copper ore on the estates of the Countess of Bridgewater in the parish of Myddle, north of Shrewsbury. Some copper ore was also obtained from Coniston in the Lake District. The copper works included a stamping mill for dressing ore, and employed cast-iron ingot moulds made in the foundry. In 1709 Darby made arrangements on behalf of a group of Bristol partners to lease the water mill on the River Tern just upstream from its confluence with the Severn, near Shrewsbury, the site of the present-day Attingham Park. An ambitious enterprise was planned, forging wrought-iron from Coalbrookdale pig-iron, rolling it into rods, hoop iron and wire, making steel, and rolling plates from brass manufactured at Coalbrookdale. One of the partners described the operation at Tern as 'the first joint work of this kind in England ... for its goodness of building Europe can't produce the like'. The term *joint works* appears to indicate that it was conceived as a mill which could fabricate both the brass and the iron which were smelted at Coalbrookdale.

Darby also secured control of the upper and middle forges in Coalbrookdale. The upper forge was a conventional finery-and-chafery works, which used pig-iron from nearby furnaces at Leighton and Kemberton, from Cheshire, the Clee Hills and the American colonies. The lower forge at Coalbrookdale, worked by the Hallen family, continued to make wrought-iron goods, particularly frying pans, supplying some handles and other parts for cast-iron ware produced by Darby and his partners.

Plate 4. Dale House, Coalbrookdale. Dale House was built by Abraham Darby I, but was incomplete at the time of his death in 1717. This photograph was taken in the 1950s when Dale House was used as a lodging house, and long before the Ironbridge Gorge Museum Trust commenced its restoration.

By 1717 Darby's interests in Shropshire had narrowed to the forges and the foundry at Coalbrookdale. The brass works seems to have been closed by 1714, when its movable equipment was sent down the Severn to Bristol. The copper works appears still to have been working when Darby died, but had probably ceased operation by 1718. The enterprise at Tern was hampered by disputes with the landlord, and by the death of the only employee able to superintend the rolling of brass plates. By 1717 the one-time joint works was no more than a finery-and-chafery forge, with a wire mill.

Darby's coke-smelting process, the most significant long-term outcome of his imaginative attempts to develop a series of works smelting and fabricating several metals in parallel, was ultimately to revolutionise the British iron industry, but it spread only slowly. It was probably tried out at one of the nearest works to Coalbrookdale about 1710, when Richard Hartshorne, who leased mines in Dawley from the Slaney family, agreed to supply coked coals to the Slaneys' furnace at Kemberton. Hartshorne was one of the principal suppliers of raw materials to Coalbrookdale, and would certainly have known about Darby's use of coke in the blast furnace. It seems that coke smelting at Kemberton was a failure, and the operators of the furnace reverted to using charcoal. In succeeding decades coke was used with less than total success at several furnaces in different parts of Britain, most of which were subsequently fired once more with charcoal.

When Abraham Darby I moved to Coalbrookdale there were no members of the Society of Friends in the immediate vicinity on the north side of the Severn, although south of the river there was a meeting house in Broseley, built in 1692, where he and his family attended meetings. Darby himself held office as clerk of monthly and preparative meetings which must have involved much travel through the Borderland region. By 1716 there were eight Quaker families in the parish of Madeley, most if not all of them linked with the Coalbrookdale ironworks. By the following year occasional Quaker meetings were being held in Coalbrookdale.

Abraham Darby's first home in Coalbrookdale was at White End, a timber-framed house which stood near the Upper Forge until it was destroyed during road widening in 1939. By 1712 he had rented Madeley Court, a Tudor mansion about a mile and a half to the east of Coalbrookdale. Soon after 1715 he began to build a new house on the western side of Coalbrookdale, over-looking the ironworks, which was sufficiently near completion in 1717 for a Quaker meeting to be held there. Abraham Darby had been ill for about two years, but was nevertheless able to attend. He did not live to occupy the house, for he died on 5 May 1717, and was buried in the Quaker graveyard at Broseley.

Rosehill House

Chapter 3

THE TRANSFORMATION OF
THE IRON INDUSTRY

ABRAHAM DARBY I's son, also called Abraham, was aged only six when his father died. He was ultimately to succeed to the management of the ironworks, and to expand their scope, but the succession was complicated. In 1717 the control of the Coalbrookdale works passed to a Bristol merchant, Thomas Goldney, to whom half of it had been mortgaged, and to Richard Ford, son-in-law of Abraham Darby I's widow, Mary. There were legal wrangles over the succession. A Quaker kinsman of Mary Darby, Joshua Sergeant, intervened on behalf of Abraham Darby II and his brothers and sisters. Without his intervention it is probable that the involvement of the Darbys with Coalbrookdale would have ceased. Mary Darby died not long after her husband and Joshua Sergeant was one of the trustees appointed to be responsible for the education of her children.

Richard Ford and Thomas Goldney began new account books when they took over the works which were kept with traditional Quaker meticulousness. Fortunately they have survived, and provide probably the most complete records of any British ironworks of the early 18th century. The main trade was in cast-iron household utensils, cooking pots, kettles, skillets and smoothing irons. They were sold to ironmongers throughout the West Midlands and the Welsh Marches, mainly through fairs. There was considerable trade with Bristol both in finished products, which were sold in bulk to a Quaker merchant called Nehemiah Champion, and in pig-iron for the city's foundries. Customers in 1718 included Richard Bromley of Bishop's Castle, Jonathan Dennal of Shrewsbury, Samuel Mason of Knighton, Miles Winstanley of Manchester, Richard Jennings of Presteigne, John Varden of Congleton, Susannah Eddows of

Macclesfield, Joseph Pearce of Ludlow, William Wood and
Francis Palmer of Birmingham, Charles Kingston of Ellesmere
and Nathan Harvey of Evesham. One regular customer, John
Ives, lived as far away as Gainsborough on the Trent, but he
was an exception, and delivery of his orders, either by road and
river via Burton, or by river and coastal shipping via Bristol, was
often difficult. Almost all the other customers lived in the West
Midlands and the Borderland, and as far as the trade in pots and
pans was concerned, the significance of Coalbrookdale in the
1720s and '30s was regional, not national.

One aspect of the work at Coalbrookdale in this period was
of more than local consequence. This was the manufacture of
cast-iron parts for steam engines. The first successful steam
engine for pumping water from mines had been erected by
Thomas Newcomen near Dudley in 1712. By 1719 there was a
similar engine at work in coal pits on the glebe land in Madeley
parish. It may well have included parts made at Coalbrookdale.
Certainly in 1718-19 three cast-iron pipes and a 'cast box' were
supplied to Stannier Parrot 'of ye Fire Engine'. Parrot was a
coalmaster, who was erecting engines for pumping water from
mines in North Warwickshire. By 1722 cylinders for steam
engines, previously made of brass, were being cast in iron at
Coalbrookdale. At least 10 were produced before 1730, and the
numbers steadily increased in the next two decades. Steam
engine parts were dispatched all over the country. In 1731 an
order was met for Alderman Ridley of Newcastle-upon-Tyne,
and other engines were supplied for coal mines near Hawarden
in Flintshire, and for lead mines at Winster in Derbyshire. The
steam engine brought the Coalbrookdale works to national
prominence.

The first iron railway wheels were cast at Coalbrookdale
during the 1720s. There had been wooden railways in the
Shropshire coalfield since the early 17th century, and the typical
operating methods of Shropshire railways had been copied in
other districts. In 1728 the coalmaster Richard Hartshorne,
supplier of many raw materials to the Darbys, was building a
railway from Little Wenlock to the banks of the Severn at
Strethill near Coalbrookdale 'for the advantage of carrying of

sand, coles, mines and minerals'. In the following year the Coalbrookdale works cast for him 18 iron railway wheels, which, as far as is known, were the first to be used on any railway in Britain. It seems likely that they were intended for vehicles running on Hartshorne's new line. In the same year the supply of iron railway wheels to other coalmasters began, and they soon became a regular part of the trade of the works.

The second Abraham Darby began to participate in the management of the ironworks in 1728 when he was 17. By the time he was of age he seems to have been acting as deputy to Richard Ford, and in 1732 a new agreement recognised that he was to enjoy a quarter of the privileges and advantages of the tenancy of the works. In 1738 he was acknowledged as a full partner. Thomas Goldney I died in 1731, but the Goldney interest in the partnership was maintained by his son, also called Thomas. The first Richard Ford died in 1745, after which his three sons retained interests in the partnership, but these were purchased by Abraham Darby II in 1756.

Somewhat surprisingly, in the 1740s, the Coalbrookdale partners became involved in the manufacture of guns. In January 1740 cannon patterns were brought to the works from Bristol, and shortly afterwards a boring-mill was built. Traditionally Quakers did not participate in the armaments trade, but without doubt the casting of cannon was carried on at Coalbrookdale until 1748, after which documentary evidence is lacking. According to the recollections recorded in 1859 of an old employee, the manufacture of guns continued until about 1790. Certainly guns were not made at Coalbrookdale during the wars with Revolutionary and Napoleonic France between 1793 and 1815.

One of the difficulties in the operation of an early 18th-century ironworks, whatever its fuel, was the securing of a sufficient supply of water to turn the waterwheels which powered the bellows. A blast furnace operated continuously and it was not possible, as with a corn-mill or a fulling-mill, simply to suspend work for a few days or weeks if water was low. Once a furnace was blown out in the spring, it had to stay out of blast until the autumn rains enabled it to be resumed without fear of another stoppage. Most ironworks therefore only worked about forty weeks of the year, ceasing operations for about three months in the summer when repairs were carried out and raw materials stockpiled. The established method of prolonging the period of work was to construct a string of pools in which water could be impounded. This had been done at Coalbrookdale before the time of Abraham Darby I, although the Darbys and their partners considerably improved the storage system. In 1735 Richard Ford applied horse pumps to return water from one of the lower pools at Coalbrookdale to the one above the upper furnace. He forecast that there would thereafter be no need to be apprehensive of water shortages. The pumps proved successful, and reduced the length of the summer break in operations. The system was improved by Abraham Darby II in 1742-3, when he constructed a steam pumping-engine to replace the horse pumps. Pits for the engine were being dug by June 1742, and a large piece of timber for the beam was acquired for £10 15s. in October. The engine house was built in December 1742 and January 1743, and the engine was set to work the following September. For more than two decades the partners at Coalbrookdale had been acquainted with the Newcomen steam engine, yet this was the first time that the engine had been applied to the making of iron. By maintaining a circuit of water between the pools the engine rendered unnecessary the cessation of work in the summer months. This was an innovation which for more than three decades provided one of the principal foundations for the development of the iron industry.

The sale of coke-blast pig-iron to forgemasters must always have been one of the ambitions of the Coalbrookdale ironmasters. Making and selling castings may have been profitable and even prestigious, but the manufacture of wrought-iron was the essential mainstream of the iron trade. The principal contribution of Abraham Darby II to the history of iron-making was that he developed ways of making pig-iron which could be used in forges, while employing coke as the fuel in his blast furnaces. There was a period of experiment in the late 1740s or early 1750s when this process was perfected. Darby's wife Abiah, writing many years later, described how her husband sent some of the pig-iron made by the new process to a forge, without revealing its origin, and when it proved to be of good quality, decided to erect new furnaces. Another account preserves a tradition that Darby spent six days and nights without sleep at the furnaces until, when iron of the desired quality was finally produced, he had to be carried home asleep by his workmen. Just what was new in the process is now difficult to understand. One of the secrets was certainly the careful selection of grades of iron ore with a low phosphorus content, but a suggestion made to Darby that he should patent his ideas perhaps indicates that the new process encompassed something more than the choice of raw materials. When the ironmaster Charles Wood visited Coalbrookdale in 1754 he found that pit coal pigs (that is, pig-iron made with coke as the fuel) were being used in the forge to make wrought-iron, and that there was such a demand for pig-iron of this sort that new furnaces were being erected to make it.

At about the same time Darby and his partners began to make use of railways. Wooden railways, as mentioned above, had long been used in the Coalbrookdale area to carry coal from mines to wharves on the banks of the Severn, but it was not until 1749 that a line was built to supply an ironworks. This was a railway built by Goldney and Ford from Coalmoor in the parish of Little Wenlock to the Coalbrookdale furnaces, and probably southwards to the wharves on the banks of the Severn. It was constructed 'for the better conveying, bringing and carrying of Cole, Ironstone or other such Materials as they shall think proper to and for the use of the Ironworks they use and occupy at Colebrook Dale'. This was the first of many lines which the partners were to build in the next hundred years.

Another new development of the 1750s was the vertical integration of ironworking concerns. Previously the Coalbrookdale partners had done no more than to operate blast furnaces and to produce for sale pig-iron and iron castings, purchasing their raw materials from local coalmasters or landowners. In the 1750s Abraham Darby II began to lease the mining rights over large tracts of land, acquiring sources of minerals which were to sustain the company for over a century.

He began a process of integration which made the ironworks in Shropshire some of the largest enterprises in Britain.

In May 1754 Darby leased the mines in the township of Great Dawley from the Slaney family, and on the same day agreed, together with Thomas Goldney II, acting in this instance as his partner, to rent from the Slaneys the Horsehay Farm in the north of Dawley parish, together with a nearby water corn-mill and its pools. Here, it was agreed, Darby and Goldney would build blast furnaces. At about the same time Darby leased mines in the manor of Ketley from Earl Gower, and built a steam engine to drain them. Darby and Goldney and their workmen transformed the landscape of the area around Horse-hay Farm. The pool in which water for driving the corn-mill was stored was not large enough for the operation of a blast furnace, whose bellows had to continue working for many months at a time. Therefore a new dam was built, and the pool greatly enlarged. The construction of the furnace with its attendant buildings was begun in the summer of 1754 when the road leading to Horsehay was busy carrying timber from Kemberton, Wrockwardine and Hadley, blocks of sandstone from Highley, firebricks from Broseley and pitch from Bridgnorth. New railways were laid to serve the works, linking it with Coal-brookdale and the Severn, with coal and iron mines in Dawley, and with limestone quarries in Little Wenlock. A steam engine was supplied from Coalbrookdale to return to the pool water which had passed over the waterwheels.

The new pool was not constructed without difficulty. It leaked water during the winter of 1754-5. At certain times a fleet of little boats could be seen upon it, with workmen on board emptying bags of charcoal and coke dust into the water to seal the leaks. In December part of the dam collapsed, and work on the project almost came to a halt. Darby had to continue to pay about sixty men for doing very little. By February labour was in short supply, one observer commenting, 'they are mustering up all that can be met, of any sort or size, old or young; none escapes them'. Many people considered that the new works at Horsehay was a reckless gamble, certain to fail, although it was well known in the district that Darby and Goldney had confidence in the project, and were determined to make it succeed however much money and however many men they might need.

Coking of coal for the furnace began as early as January 1755, perhaps because coke dust was needed to plug the leaks in the pool rather than because coke was being stockpiled. The pumping engine began work in April, and the first load of iron ore from the mines in Lawley arrived on 1 May. Two weeks afterwards the furnace was in blast and making iron, and confounded the pessimistic critics of the project. It was soon making an average of 15 tons of pig-iron a week, and as much as 22 tons in a good week. This was the first time that a coke-fired furnace had been proved conclusively superior to one fired with charcoal. Most of the pig-iron from Horsehay was sold to forgemasters, much of it to the Knight and Foley families who controlled the principal iron-making partnerships in the West Midlands.

Plate 5. Sunniside, the house built by Abraham Darby II about 1750, which stood amongst ornamental grounds that included a small deer park. This very early photograph shows the house shortly before it was demolished in 1856.

The Seven Years War broke out in 1756, the year after the Horsehay blast furnace went into production. The demand for munitions, together with restrictions on the importation of foreign iron, increased the price of iron in England. Darby's success in using coke to make forge pig-iron was soon copied. In April 1756 Darby and Goldney agreed to erect a second blast furnace at Horsehay, and in October of that year they leased 14 acres of land called the Allmoores in the manor of Ketley for the construction of two further furnaces. A series of pools was constructed in the valley of the Ketley Brook, and a steam engine was installed to recirculate water. In 1759 Darby leased a tract of land in Lawley which came to be known as the Newdale estate. The partners were facing difficulties over their leases at Coalbrookdale at this time, and it seems likely that they planned to relocate their furnaces and foundry at Newdale. Extensive archaeological investigations in 1987 show that a foundry was constructed, and possibly a blast furnace, but the venture was short-lived. A long terrace of back-to-back cottages came to be largely occupied by miners, while one of the industrial buildings was put to use as a Quaker meeting house.

Other partnerships were anxious to erect ironworks in the district. In 1757 the New Willey Company, in which the celebrated John Wilkinson was a partner, took over the ancient Willey furnace near Broseley on the estates of the Forester family. They constructed a second furnace on a different site, close to the present-day Broseley-Much Wenlock road. At Lightmoor and at Madeley Wood, two partnerships which were essentially combinations of local master colliers built pairs of blast furnaces in 1757-8. In all, nine blast furnaces were built within four miles of Coalbrookdale in the four years between 1755 and 1758. For the rest of the 18th century it was to remain the principal iron-making district in Great Britain.

There is little evidence to throw light on day-to-day happenings during this most important period of the history of the Shropshire iron industry. Abiah Darby, the wife of Abraham Darby II, has left a lengthy journal, but it is largely concerned

Plate 6. The Old Row, Horsehay. This terrace was built in several phases from the mid-1750s to accommodate workers at the adjacent Horsehay furnaces. A century later it was still occupied predominantly by skilled ironworkers. It now forms part of a conservation area.

with religious matters. One occasion which she does describe is the blowing in of the second blast furnace at Horsehay:

> We...dined upwards of 300 people so that our Family that day was large with the poor folks besides. We killed a fat Cow, and the fatted Calf: hams: and 10 large puddings full of fruit: and 2 hogs heads of drink. We carried it up in Railway Wagons and had 4 tables spread under covers.

The achievement of the first Abraham Darby was to succeed where others had failed in smelting iron ore with mineral fuel instead of charcoal. His son's achievements were those of a co-ordinator rather than an inventor, a deviser of systems rather than processes. He accomplished what Richard Arkwright was to achieve in the cotton trade some years later; he put together a series of ideas, most of which were probably not his own, and gained from them something more than a mere sum of the parts. By experiment he found out how to make forge pig-iron using coke. He put together Richard Ford's idea of recycling the water from the furnace pools with the knowledge of the workings of steam engines gained at Coalbrookdale through building them, and achieved a water-power system by which ironworks could be almost independent of rainfall. He adapted the long-established Shropshire railway to supply materials to ironworks. He realised that to secure supplies of raw materials it was necessary for ironmasters to lease large tracts of land and to organise themselves the operations of the mines. At Horsehay and Ketley all these ideas were synthesised. Land was leased, and Darby sank pits and installed steam engines to keep them free from water. From the pits ore and coal were taken by railway to the furnaces. At the blast furnaces the ore was reduced to pig-iron, which was taken by railway to the Severn, along which barges and trows conveyed it to customers. Darby gained positive enjoyment from seeing his projects come to fruition. His wife wrote in 1757, 'My husband delights in laying out money: and when he'll stop I don't know'. Darby was not ashamed of the profit motive. He told Goldney with some pride in 1756 that the first Horsehay furnace was making as much as 22 tons of iron a week, 'sold off as fast as made at profit enough, will soon find money enough for the furnace and for the pocket too'.

Like his father, Abraham Darby II was active in the affairs of the Society of Friends, and it was during his time that regular meetings were established in Coalbrookdale. A graveyard was enclosed for the use of members of the Society, and it was there that he was buried when he died on 31 March 1763 at the age of fifty-one. His wife described him thus:

> Just in his dealings, of universal benevolence and Charity, living Strictly to the Rectitude of the Divine and moral Law, held forth by his great Lord and Saviour, ... had an Extraordinary Command over his own Spirit, which thru' the assistance of Divine Grace enabled him to bear up with fortitude above all opposition.

Chapter 4

COALBROOKDALE AT ITS ZENITH

WHEN ABRAHAM DARBY II died in 1763, his son, the third Abraham, was aged only eleven. Responsibility for the management of the Coalbrookdale enterprises was assumed by Richard Reynolds, a member of a Bristol Quaker family who had moved to Shropshire in 1756 to represent the interests of Thomas Goldney II. The following year he married Hannah, daughter of Abraham Darby II. At about the same time he took a third share with his father-in-law and Thomas Goldney II in the Ketley ironworks. Reynolds established his home at Ketley Bank House. Richard Reynolds' eldest son William, grandson of Abraham Darby II, who was to prove the most imaginative of the 18th-century Shropshire ironmasters, was born in 1758. Hannah Reynolds died in 1762, and in December 1763 Richard Reynolds married his second wife, Rebecca Gulson of Coventry.

Several important developments in the affairs of the Coalbrookdale partnership took place under the direction of Richard Reynolds in the 1760s. In 1764 mining leases on the lands of Earl Gower in Ketley and Donnington were renegotiated. The Donnington Wood and Wrockwardine Wood mines in the north of the Shropshire coalfield were sources of ore for the furnaces at Ketley and Horsehay. In 1767 iron rails were used for the first time on the partnership's railways. For some time previously two-level wooden rails had been employed, with the advantage that when the top section was worn out by traffic, it could be replaced without disturbing the track bed. Reynolds' first iron rails were thin strips of cast iron, about 6 ft. by 3¼ in. by 1¼ in., which replaced the upper levels of the two-level wooden rails. Iron rails were used on many of the partnership's railways. In 1768 they began to be cast at Horsehay in considerable

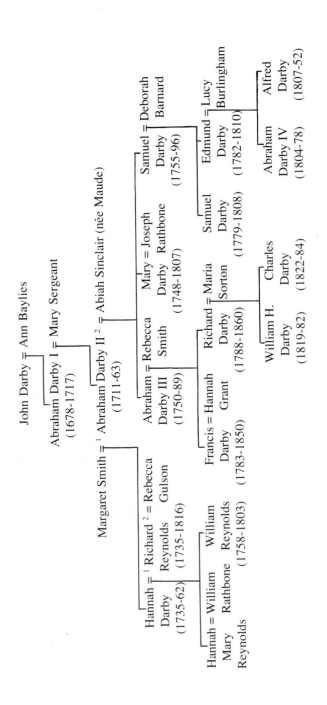

Fig. 1. The Darby Family Tree (Simplified)

numbers, and by 1785 Richard Reynolds calculated that the partnership was operating about twenty route miles of iron railways.

Reynolds was also concerned with the attempt made by the brothers George and Thomas Cranage to make wrought-iron from pig-iron in a reverberatory furnace using coke rather than the charcoal used in the conventional finery-and-chafery forge. The brothers took out a patent in 1766, and the following year the young Joseph Banks saw the process demonstrated at the Upper Forge, Coalbrookdale. It proved wasteful in its consumption of pig-iron and was abandoned, although it formed an essential element of the sequence of operations which Henry Cort synthesised as the puddling process for making wrought-iron in 1784.

The third Abraham Darby began to work at Coalbrookdale in 1768, when he was eighteen. The partners' concerns then comprised three ironworks, Coalbrookdale and Horsehay, each with two blast furnaces, and Ketley with three, forges at Coalbrookdale and Bridgnorth, leases on tracts of mining land extending from Donnington in the north of the Shropshire coalfield to the River Severn, and several farms in Madeley. During Darby's lifetime the company's activities expanded considerably. The survival of his personal account books means that it is possible to discover more about the details of his life and interests than those of his father and grandfather, although the few surviving works records for this period are concerned solely with activities at Horsehay.

During the lifetime of Abraham Darby III another great Quaker mercantile family, the Rathbones of Liverpool became involved in the affairs of the Coalbrookdale Company. In 1771, when Darby was only just of age, he had a quarter interest in the ship *Darby* which was sailing from Liverpool to Danzig (Gdansk), returning with cargoes of timber. He remitted his share of the capital in the enterprise through Joseph Rathbone, who had married Darby's sister, Mary, in 1768. In 1786 Hannah, the daughter of Richard Reynolds by his first wife, sister of William Reynolds and grand-daughter of Abraham Darby II, was married to William Rathbone. During the 1780s parts of the

Coalbrookdale concerns were mortgaged to the Rathbones, and in 1783 Joseph Rathbone was partner with William Reynolds in the establishment of a new ironworks at Donnington Wood. The interests of the Darbys, Reynoldses and Rathbones in the 1770s, '80s and '90s were closely intermixed. For the purposes of this study their various partnerships will be treated as a single concern until their formal separation in 1795. In the time of Abraham Darby III the partnership was probably the largest iron-making concern in Britain.

The Coalbrookdale partnership shared to the full the prosperity of the Shropshire iron industry in the late 1770s and early 1780s. In 1776 Abraham Darby III purchased the Bedlam or Madeley Wood blast furnaces on the banks of the Severn which had been built in 1757-8. Among the properties on the site was a range of tar ovens, one of the earliest in the district. Darby ceased to use the ovens about 1779, although at a later date further coke and tar ovens on the principles of Lord Dundonald were built at Madeley Wood. At the same time the Coalbrookdale partners took over the associated Madeley Field coalworks, a group of pits where they encountered considerable problems in the ensuing years, particularly from the explosive gas, methane, known to the miners as fire damp.

Two blast furnaces were built at Donnington Wood on land belonging to Earl Gower in 1783 and 1785. The Coalbrookdale forges were enlarged in 1776, and in the early 1780s a forge was built at Horsehay, initially water-powered but later worked by steam engines. This forge came to specialise in rolling wrought-iron plates for boilers. A forge at Ketley, steam-powered from the first, came into production in 1785.

The Coalbrookdale partners had many contacts with Matthew Boulton and James Watt, whose first improved steam engines were set to work in 1776, the second of them at John Wilkinson's Willey ironworks. Between 1778 and 1780 two Boulton & Watt engines were installed at the Ketley ironworks, and in 1781-2 the Newcomen pumping engine at Coalbrookdale was replaced by a Boulton & Watt engine named *Resolution*, probably the largest steam engine to be constructed in the 18th

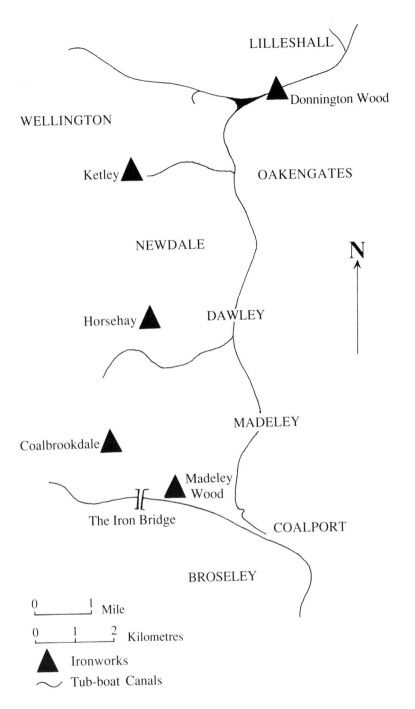

Fig. 2. The Shropshire ironworks of the Derby-
Reynolds-Rathbone partnerships, *c*.1790.

century. Like other ironmasters, the Coalbrookdale partners installed many other steam engines in the mines and ironworks during the 1780s and '90s, until by 1800 there were about two hundred engines working in the Shropshire coalfield.

The partners leased new tracts of mining land, and set up warehouses in Liverpool, London and elsewhere. An increasing interest was taken in limestone mining and quarrying, since limestone was used as a flux in iron-making, and supplies were limited.

Abraham Darby was closely involved in the working of the Madeley, Sunniside and Hay farms, which provided the ironmasters with bases for the many horses needed to operate railways and for the formation of teams to draw road waggons. Occupying farmland could simplify the building of new railways by making it easier to obtain way-leaves. It also provided iron-

Plate 7. An Afternoon View of Coalbrookdale by William Williams, 1777. This view of Coalbrookdale from Lincoln Hill, was painted at the time when plans were being made for casting the ribs of the Iron Bridge. It shows clearly the pools, which provided water-power for the works, the steam engine which recirculated water between them, and heaps of coal being coked.

masters with some influence in the local grain trade, enabling them to reduce the risk of riots by workpeople in times of food shortage, by ensuring that grain was not sold out of the district. Sunniside Farm was used to supply horses for the works. Darby's accounts show occasional purchases of horses (for example, from Lichfield Fair in 1774) and of large quantities of oats, hay, bran and hurdles. Teams of horses were supplied to take goods in waggons from the ironworks to such destinations as Chester, Bedworth, Brownhills and Calves Heath (near Gailey, Staffs.). The Hay Farm was operated in a more conventional way, and Darby invested considerable sums in its improvement. In 1772-3 bricks were made on the spot for the construction of new buildings, for which lime, timber and tiles were delivered. Many fruit trees were planted and new cattle were acquired. By 1776 Darby was growing clover on the farm, and his sources of income from it included the sale of wheat, barley, sheep, horses and bark, the latter doubtless for tanning.

Abraham Darby III's chief claim to fame arises from this role in the building of the Iron Bridge. Of the many innovations in the making and use of iron made in Shropshire in the 18th century, the building of the bridge, universally regarded at the time as the first to be built of iron, was the one which most captured the imagination of contemporaries and which still attracts visitors.

For two centuries before the time of Abraham Darby III the Severn Gorge had been a busy area, with a population of miners, potters, boat-builders, bargemen and ironworkers along the banks of the river in the parishes of Benthall, Broseley and Madeley. There was no bridge across the Severn in the Gorge. The nearest was at Buildwas, about a mile and a half upstream from Coalbrookdale, but to approach this bridge from the downstream side on the south bank was difficult because of the limestone cliffs on Benthall Edge. Downstream the nearest bridge was at Bridgnorth, too far away to be of use to anyone wanting to cross from Broseley to Madeley. Passengers were carried over the river in the Gorge by several ferries, but these could be dangerous at times of flood. Heavy commodities like

iron ore and limestone were regularly conveyed across the
river, probably by barges waiting between voyages to distant
destinations.

Proposals to construct a bridge between Madeley and
Broseley or Benthall had been made from the middle of the 18th
century, but the steepness of the banks, the difficulty of providing adequate approaches and the density of shipping on the
Severn had prevented progress. The project which was to
culminate in the building of the Iron Bridge began, in a formal
sense, in September 1775 when a group of interested people
met at the house of Abraham Cannadine, a cooper and probably
an innkeeper, in Broseley. They decided that a bridge should be
built with its northern end by the house of Thomas Crumpton, in
what was then called Madeley Wood. Its southern terminus was
to be in Benthall, west of the brook which divided that parish
from Broseley. Abraham Darby III did not attend the meeting,
but was appointed treasurer to the project, a post which he held
until its completion.

Abraham Darby III and his brother Samuel were the only
members of the Coalbrookdale partnerships to be involved with
the bridge project at its outset. John Wilkinson of the Willey ironworks was also a partner, together with Edward Blakeway,
once a Shrewsbury draper, but by 1775 also a partner in the
Willey works, and later one of the founders of the porcelain
works at Coalport. Other subscribers included Edward Harries,
owner of the Benthall estate and John Thursfield, a member of a
Jackfield earthenware manufacturing family.

Another partner was a Shrewsbury architect, Thomas
Farnolls Pritchard. It was he who was instructed at the first
meeting to prepare a design for a bridge. Pritchard had taken an
interest in the use of iron for bridges before this date. In October
1775 he completed a plan for an iron bridge of four ribs,
spanning 120 ft. Together with Abraham Darby he calculated
the cost of the structure, and concluded that it could be built for
£3,200, without any allowance for land costs. Abraham Darby
agreed to erect the bridge, but the proprietors withdrew their
instructions to him to do so in May 1776, when they advertised
for anyone who would be willing to build a single-arch bridge,
'of stone, brick or timber'. The response was apparently

disappointing, for in June 1776 they again agreed to construct an iron bridge to Pritchard's design. In the autumn it was confirmed that Darby should build a structure with a span of 120 ft. No work was done, and the following summer Darby came to another agreement with the subscribers, that he should build a bridge of 90-ft. span. It seems that this was the design, modified to include a towpath so that the span was 100 ft. 6 in., which was finally followed. In December 1777 Thomas Farnolls Pritchard died. He remained a subscriber to the project up to the time of his death, and probably made a substantial contribution to the final design of the bridge. Two years later his brother was paid nearly £40 on account of his work, and the ogee and circle motifs which decorate the bridge are typical of his style. While Pritchard's contribution was considerable, it is perhaps inappropriate to look for a single designer of any project as innovative as the Iron Bridge. It was Abraham Darby III who was responsible for building the bridge, and confronting the numerous problems which arose during the period of construction.

In November 1776 one of the Darby family wrote to a kinswoman in Sunderland:

> The Bridge, that is to be made over the Severn at the bottom of the Dale is now fix'd upon to be an *Iron* one, wch. certainly when compleated will be one of the great curiosities yt this Nation or any other can boast of ... I suppose it will all be cast in the Dale for Cousin Abram. will have the whole direction.

To what extent Darby controlled the project is indicated in his personal cash books and ledgers. Mixed with the records of his farming activities, his investments and even his petty household expenses, are the accounting entries which reveal the chronology of the erection of the first iron bridge.

Some work was done on the road running up the valley of the Benthall brook from the south end of the projected bridge in the summer of 1777, but it was not until November of that year that regular work began on the project, and even then, during the winter months, only a few men were employed. The accounts suggest that between 20 and 30 men worked on the bridge during the summer and autumn of 1778, augmented by groups of day labourers brought in for short spells. An ale-

Plate 8. The Iron Bridge from the north bank of the River Severn.

drinking at the end of October probably celebrated the completion of a significant stage. Fewer men were employed while
the river was high during the winter months. In the spring of
1779 it seems that Darby's workmen were preparing to erect
the ironwork, and by the end of March most of the parts were
probably laid out on the banks of the Severn ready for erection.
Quantities of scaffold timber and ropes were purchased, and the
number of workmen employed steadily increased. A barge was
hired, and on 1 and 2 July the first pair of ribs was hauled into
place. The completion of the main structure went ahead quite
quickly, and was probably celebrated by the spending of nine
guineas on ale on 23 October. The scaffolding was taken down
the following month.

The main part of the bridge was now completed, but it was
not until New Year's Day 1781 that it was opened to traffic. One
cause of the delay was the need to wait for the completion of
access roads, particularly on the north bank. It is also possible
that the abutments were not completed until after the ironwork
was in place. About twenty men were employed on the project
during most of 1780. The cost of erecting the bridge came to
£2,737 4s. 4d., a much greater sum than the estimate of 1775
which suggested that only £550 would be needed for this

purpose. Less is known about the manufacture of the parts of the bridge. Most evidence suggests that Abraham Darby III enlarged the old furnace at Coalbrookdale in 1777 in order to provide sufficient ironmaking capacity to manufacture the ribs of the bridge. The Iron Bridge contains nearly 400 tons of castings, equivalent to the output of a blast furnace of the period for three or four months. Neither the cost of the iron ribs, nor that of the stonework used in the abutments is known, nor is there any record of the expenditure incurred on materials for the roads built by the bridge proprietors, nor even of the cost of the land used for the project.

The bridge proprietors realised before the Iron Bridge was opened to traffic that it would be an attraction for visitors. Drawings of the structure were advertised for sale in June 1780, and in January 1781 Darby's accounts reveal that Michael Angelo Rooker, scene painter at the Haymarket Theatre, was brought to Shropshire to draw the bridge. Engravings of Rooker's drawing were advertised the following May. In October 1780 Darby commissioned a painting of the bridge by William Williams, a Shrewsbury artist, who three years earlier had painted two celebrated pictures of Coalbrookdale.

The order of assembly of the parts of the Iron Bridge was probably rehearsed with a model. If such a model was used, it is probably now lost, although it may have been sold to Sir Edward Smythe of Acton Burnell, who, in 1782, paid two Shrewsbury heraldic painters to paint what was apparently a large model of the bridge. In 1783, Thomas Gregory, who had supervised the last stages of the erection of the bridge, made a model in mahogany, which was presented to the Society of Arts, and is now in the Science Museum, London. Two years later, 'sensible of the magnitude and importance of the Iron Bridge', the Society of Arts presented Abraham Darby with their gold medal.

Abraham and Samuel Darby were concerned with the building of the *Tontine* Hotel, the imposing hostelry which faces the north end of the Iron Bridge. Other shareholders in the project included Richard and William Reynolds, John Wilkinson and Joseph Rathbone. John Hiram Haycock of Shrewsbury was employed as architect, and it seems likely that Abraham Darby was commissioned by the subscribers to overlook the construction of the building. The hotel was opened in 1784, but it was not wholly successful, and the original subscribers sold it seven years later.

The building of the Iron Bridge changed the pattern of roads in the Gorge. Abraham Darby III was already connected with the administration of roads before the beginning of the bridge project. He and his brother Samuel were trustees of the Wenlock turnpike trust, which was responsible for a network of roads radiating from the town of Much Wenlock, including the route down Farley Dingle to Buildwas Bridge, along which the Shropshire ironmasters brought loads of limestone from Wenlock Edge for their blast furnaces. Darby's accounts show that he sent £20 to the trust in 1779 towards the cost of obtaining the Act of Parliament necessary for renewing its powers. Abraham and Samuel Darby were also trustees of the road from Tern Bridge on Watling Street to Coalbrookdale, for which an Act of Parliament was obtained in 1778. The purpose of this road, formed from several straggling country lanes in the parishes of Wroxeter, Eaton Constantine, Leighton and Buildwas, was to give direct access from Shrewsbury to the Iron Bridge. When it was formally opened to traffic in 1779 many of its first users were sightseers going to look at the half-completed Iron Bridge. The road was always called the Leighton turnpike, since its only toll gate was by the bridge in the village of Leighton.

Darby was also active in the administration of the Madeley turnpike trust, whose roads, turnpiked in 1764, were in the shape of a distorted letter 'X', with one section going from the *Buck's Head* at Wellington, by way of Lawley Bank, Dawley, Madeley and Sutton Maddock to Beckbury and the New Inns on the Staffordshire border, and the other, from a junction with the Leighton turnpike near Coalbrookdale, through Madeley, to Kemberton. The two sections crossed at the *Cuckoo Oak* public house in Madeley. In 1776 Darby agreed to act as surveyor for the portions of the road in Madeley parish. At this time surveyors of roads were not formally qualified engineers, but practical men who could be trusted to carry out such simple repairs as the income of the trusts allowed, and who could oversee the collection of tolls and the maintenance of sign posts. In 1780 the road between the *Cuckoo Oak* and the Madeley parish boundary had fallen into a bad state, and it was Darby who saw that it was repaired. From 1782 Darby's duties lapsed when the trustees appointed a professional surveyor, William Dukes, to oversee the whole system. Darby continued to attend meetings as a trustee, as did his brother Samuel, and his son Francis, after his death. Abraham Darby III's position as a respected member of the trust did not always protect him from rebukes for damage done to the roads by the Coalbrookdale Company's waggons. In 1776, for example, the turnpike clerk was instructed to write to him complaining about the damage caused by traffic to and from Darby's limestone works on Lincoln Hill.

The Severn Navigation was the main means by which iron and iron products from the Coalbrookdale district were sent to other parts of Britain. For many months in most years low water made it impossible for barges to operate. In 1772 Abraham Darby III paid two and a half guineas to George Young, a Worcester surveyor, for a plan of the river from Coalbrookdale to Bewdley. This may well have been in connection with an Act of Parliament obtained in that year for the building of a towpath, but it was more than 20 years before the provisions of the Act were implemented. When towpaths were finally built, the Darbys took an active role in their administration. Edward Darby, for example, was a trustee of the Coalbrookdale-Shrewsbury path, authorised in 1809.

The other major development in the transport facilities of the Shropshire coalfield in the 1780s was the building of the Shropshire Canal, the first of the tub-boat canals in the county to be authorised by an Act of Parliament. The local canal system originated in the mid-1760s when Earl Gower and the brothers Thomas and John Gilbert built the Donnington Wood Canal on the Earl's Lilleshall estate, but this and two other short canals built before 1788 were private waterways on private land. In 1788 an Act was obtained for the Shropshire Canal, which was to extend from Donnington Wood, where there was a junction with two of the earlier waterways, to Southall Bank on the borders of Dawley and Madeley, from where there were to be two lines to the Severn, one to the Styches Weir, Coalbrookdale, and the other to some riverside meadows belonging to the Hay

Farm. The line to Styches Weir was built only as far as Brierly Hill above Coalbrookdale. In the meadows around the other terminus grew up the 'new town' of Coalport, with wharves, china factories, chain works and rows of trim workers' cottages. Shortly before the construction of the canal began Abraham Darby sold the site of Coalport to the Reynolds family. Abraham Darby was not a shareholder in the Shropshire Canal, and died before it was completed, but his brother Samuel owned shares in the company to the value of £500, and at the first subscribers' meeting in June 1788 he was appointed treasurer to the company.

The genius behind the Shropshire tub-boat canal system was William Reynolds, cousin of Abraham Darby III and grandson of Abraham Darby II. He surveyed the route, and overlooked the construction of the canal. The first of the six inclined planes, for which the Shropshire canals are famous, was built on Reynolds' private canal at Ketley. He was closely involved with the development of the modified type used on the Shropshire Canal at Wrockwardine Wood, Windmill Farm and the Hay, which was based on a design put forward in a competition by Henry Williams and John Loudon.

Abraham Darby III's accounts give an impression of the quality of life in his household. Darby employed a considerable number of household servants and the house must have presented a luxurious appearance. Carpets worth over £25 were bought in March 1776 and over £60 was spent on plate the same month. He also purchased pewter, various silver items, some glass salvers and a glass lamp. In 1776 he bought a red leather hat box from Bristol, and, in the following year, a wig. He obtained such items as hats, shoes and stockings on visits to London, and sometimes from Shrewsbury. Newspapers and magazines were regularly purchased. Bread was normally bought from one Robert Horton, usually costing between £1 and £2 per month. Cocoa and chocolate were purchased periodically from Joseph Fry, the Quaker chocolate maker in Bristol. Wine came regularly from one John Flint, and in 1779 Samuel Jones was paid 'For Cyder &c. kepd for me'. In 1777 Darby was the owner of a white and yellow spaniel bitch called Juno and a reddish brown dog called 'Seeker', both of which were lost in Benthall Edge woods.

Like his ancestors, Abraham Darby III was active in the Society of Friends, and the money collected at various Quaker meetings was scrupulously recorded in his account books. A new Quaker meeting house was established at Newdale in the 1760s, but in 1778 the meeting house in Broseley was given up. Meetings in Coalbrookdale were probably better attended than at any other period. Darby left provision in his will for the maintenance of the meeting house and the nearby graveyard.

During the lifetime of Abraham Darby III the area around Coalbrookdale became the most celebrated industrial region in Great Britain. Engineers and manufacturers flocked there to examine newly-evolved technologies. Journalists, social commentaters, artists and simple seekers after the curious and spectacular were attracted by the extraordinary landscape of pit headstocks, waste tips and blazing furnaces. It was also a time of intellectual excitement. Few of the innovations of the Industrial Revolution which involved the use of iron had no connections with the Coalbrookdale area. The Darbys and Reynoldses were in contact with Matthew Boulton and James Watt, pioneers of the steam engine. They had links with John Wilkinson, who had at different times four ironworks in Shropshire, and was associated with the Iron Bridge, the Shropshire Canal and various turnpike roads. Lord Dundonald, pioneer of the distillation of coal tar and of alkali manufacture, had coke and tar works at Calcutts and Benthall, and must have met the Darbys through his friendship with Richard and William Reynolds, at whose tables he often dined. William Jessop, the most eminent canal engineer of the late 18th century, visited Shropshire to give advice on the improvement of the Severn and the route of the Shropshire Canal. John Loudon McAdam, the road engineer, had connections with Shropshire turnpike trusts, and on one occasion visited Lord Dundonald in Shropshire. John Curr, pioneer of the plateway and a talented mining engineer, advised the Coalbrookdale partners in the early 1790s. Henry Cort, inventor of the puddling process for making wrought-iron in 1784, demonstrated it at Ketley the same year. Thomas Telford grew to know the Coalbrookdale area after he became

surveyor to the county of Shropshire in 1787, and in old age he
would travel from Wolverhampton to Shrewsbury by way of the
Ironbridge Gorge simply to show the sights to colleagues.

This was a time of intellectual and scientific ferment when
new ideas in science and technology were eagerly discussed in
Shropshire. Abraham Darby III shared this interest in science.
In 1771 he purchased a camera obscura and an 'electrical
machine', together with some books, for a total cost of nearly
£17. Like many ironmasters he was interested in geology.
Erasmus Darwin, the Lichfield physician and botanist, and
grandfather of Charles Darwin, recorded that Darby sent him
some fragments of lead ore which he had found in limestone
strata near Coalbrookdale.

Abraham Darby III was only 39 when he died. Through his
talents the project to build the Iron Bridge had been realised.
Had he lived through the 1790s the innovations carried out in the
Ironbridge Gorge, most of them associated with his cousin
William Reynolds, might well have been even more remarkable.

Chapter 5

THE WAR-TIME YEARS

ABRAHAM DARBY III died in 1789 at the age of 39, and his brother Samuel at the age of 41 in 1796. Again there was an uneasy interregnum. Abraham's eldest son Francis was aged only six in 1789, and when Samuel died his son Edmund was only fourteen. By this time the pattern of Darby-Reynolds-Rathbone partnerships had grown unwieldy, and the Darby share in the enterprises was insecure. Many of the family's assets were mortgaged to Richard Reynolds or to the Rathbones, and the Reynoldses had purchased from the Darbys the Lordship of the Manor of Madeley and the meadows which became the site of the 'new town' of Coalport. In 1793 the partners were worried about the 'general unprofitable and unproductive nature of the concerns', and the following year the predominance of women among the shareholders was given as the reason for attempting to sell off such of the works as could easily be detached from the rest. The Coalbrookdale Company's reputation for the quality of its products was now sullied. The correspondence of Boulton & Watt in the late 1790s and early 1800s contains many complaints about slow deliveries from Coalbrookdale and defects in the castings supplied. In June 1796 the interests of the Darby and Reynolds families in the associated works in Shropshire were separated. The Reynoldses took full control of the Ketley and Madeley Wood ironworks and their associated mines, and the Darbys took Coalbrookdale and Horsehay, retaining for themselves the right to trade as 'the Coalbrookdale Company'. The Donnington Wood blast furnaces were sold in 1796 to John Bishton, who, in 1802, took them into the Lilleshall Company. Various small concerns which had belonged to the partnership were sold or taken over by individual members of the two families. The controlling shareholders of the Coalbrookdale Company were now the surviving daughters of Abraham Darby II, Deborah Darby, widow of Samuel, and Rebecca Darby, widow of Abraham III. Richard Dearman, brother of Richard Reynolds' daughter-in-law, was works manager from 1794 until 1894, and Mark Gilpin the works clerk.

The fortunes of the Coalbrookdale Company revived gradually from the late 1790s. From 1803 Edmund Darby, son of Samuel, was in charge of the works. Bridge building became a significant part of the Company's activities. For over a decade after its completion, the Iron Bridge remained a solitary curiosity, but by the early 1790s various people were preparing designs for iron bridges, among them the architect John Nash and the political philosopher Tom Paine. In 1791 the Coalbrookdale Company constructed a finely ornamented bridge in Trentham Park near Stoke on Trent, one of the homes of the Marquess of Stafford, and in the same year castings for a bridge were exported to the Netherlands. The best advertisement for iron bridges was an exceptional flood on the Severn in February 1795, which severely damaged every bridge

Plate 9. A bridge across the Kennet and Avon Canal in Sydney Gardens, Bath, cast by the Coalbrookdale Company in 1800.

over the river except the Iron Bridge, which, according to one newspaper, 'firmly stood and dauntless braved the storm'. Almost immediately the Coalbrookdale Company began to supply castings for other iron bridges. It produced the castings for Thomas Telford's bridge built for the county authorities at Buildwas, replacing a medieval structure swept away in the flood. By the end of 1795 two other bridges were being made at Coalbrookdale, one for Cound, near Shrewsbury, and one for Bridgwater in Somerset. In 1797 a bridge with a 36-ft. span was completed for erection at Cound Arbour. It is now the oldest iron bridge still open to normal traffic. In September 1797 John Nash's second iron bridge at Stanford on Teme in Worcestershire was completed, using ironwork from Coalbrookdale. His first bridge at Stanford had collapsed in 1795 a fortnight after it was built, and the Coalbrookdale Company had issued a disclaimer of responsibility for it. A succession of other bridges followed, including two for the Bristol Docks Company supplied in 1805, together with a steam engine, and a 50-ton bridge exported to Jamaica in 1907.

Many steam engines were manufactured at Coalbrookdale in the 1790s and 1800s. Some were to the design of James Watt, and were built under licence, but other types were constructed, some designed by engineers endeavouring to circumvent the patents which protected Watt's designs until 1800. Of the engineers associated with Coalbrookdale at this time, the most eminent was the Cornishman, Richard Trevithick. He was not merely trying to bypass the Watt patents, but was an innovator who contributed as much to the development of steam power as Watt himself. The Trevithick family's connection with Coalbrookdale extended through several decades, for Richard Trevithick's father, also Richard, had visited the works to order iron parts for Newcomen engines which he was erecting in Cornwall. The younger Trevithick first went to Coalbrookdale in 1796. In 1802 he built a high-pressure experimental engine there, and before the end of the year constructed the first steam railway locomotive to run on a plateway at Coalbrookdale. It seems that this locomotive was never put to work, although its components were retained, preserved and revered at Coalbrookdale for more than 70 years. The first of Trevithick's locomotives which is known to have drawn a load was that which was set to work at Penydarren near Merthyr in 1804. Trevithick maintained close connections with Coalbrookdale and in the first decade of the 19th century several engines to his designs were supplied to customers in various parts of Britain. In 1804 consideration was given to the erection of a high-pressure engine to drive a corn-mill at Worcester. This may have been the 18-inch engine sold to John Burlingham, a relation of Edmund Darby's wife, in the following year. Also in 1804 an engine on Trevithick's principles was built at Coalbrookdale for a textile mill in Macclesfield. Trevithick used it to experiment with the application of steam power to a barge on the Severn.

Coalbrookdale was one of the country's leading suppliers of steam engines in this period, although not all were as advanced as the Trevithick engines. Even after the expiry of James Watt's patents in 1800 some customers continued to order Newcomen or 'common' atmospheric engines, like the 26-inch 'engine on the common plan' supplied to R. Rowlands & Co. in May 1805.

An important innovation in the architectural use of cast-iron was the glass and iron roof of the picture gallery at Attingham Park near Shrewsbury. The house at Attingham was built by George Steuart for the first Lord Berwick in 1783-5, and was enlarged by John Nash in 1805-7. The Coalbrookdale Company's part in the work is revealed by a letter from one of the works agents to Edmund Darby in April 1806, in which he mentioned that a Mr. Peploe of Herefordshire wanted 'some cast-iron arches like those you did for Lord Berwick'. Cast-iron window frames were also being produced at Coalbrookdale. In 1793-5 frames in the Gothic style were cast for St Alkmund's Church, Shrewsbury. Windows were provided in 1801 for St Peter's, Adderley near Market Drayton, and in 1811 an order was fulfilled for windows for Aske Hall in North Yorkshire.

Apart from bridges, steam engines and architectural iron-works, the products of Coalbrookdale about 1800 were astonishingly varied. For other industries the works cast stamp heads for the dressing plants at Cornish tin mines, anvil blocks, power-mill beds for making gunpowder, lathe frames and sugar rolls. For farmers they made cones and shieldboards for ploughs, milk pans and cider and cheese presses. An assortment of household goods was produced: bedsteads, book cases, clock weights, cranes for kitchen fireplaces, kettles, frying pans, shoe scrapers, grates, stoves and ovens. One product which survives is a meticulously-cast register chest specially made for St John's church, Ditton Priors, in 1814. It is possible that such variety was detrimental to the prosperity of the works, for a memorandum written about 1800 suggested that the difficulties of costing so many different items, as well as the remoteness of Coalbrookdale from the most productive mines and the consequent high transport costs, made the foundry the least profitable of the Coalbrookdale Company's concerns. The two ancient and water-powered blast furnaces were used almost exclusively to make iron for use in the associated foundry shops, and were surrounded by dense complexes of pattern shops, moulding rooms, air furnaces and cupolas for re-melting the pig-iron. In September 1801 there was an explosion at the Old Furnace when water leaked in during a storm, and it may well have been to keep up production while this furnace was being

Plate 10. A whaling pot inscribed 'Coalbrookdale', photographed in Hawaii. The flattened edges of the whaling pots prevented them from rotating against each other when they were used for holding whale blubber on the decks of ships. Similar pots have been located in other parts of the Pacific Ocean, while some never left Coalbrookdale where they were used as domestic water butts.

rebuilt that the adjacent small 'snapper furnace' was constructed.

The products of the Horsehay works were less varied. Much of the pig-iron from the furnaces was sent to forges in north Worcestershire and south Staffordshire, a pattern of trade established in the 1750s, but a considerable amount went to the forges at Horsehay itself, and was ultimately sold as wrought-iron bar or plate. A speciality was the production of wrought-iron boilers which were sold to steam engine users all over the Midlands.

The first decade of the 19th century, the period of the Napoleonic Wars, was a time of prosperity for the iron trade generally, and the Darby family's concerns shared this prosperity to the full, although they took no part in the armaments trade. In May 1805 a third blast furnace went into production at Horsehay. A not very literate clerk scrawled 'whent of Verry Well' in one of the account books. Alterations to the forges went on almost continuously, and by 1808 most of Horsehay's wrought-iron was being made by Henry Cort's puddling process, although in the 1790s the 'stamping and potting' process patented by the West Bromwich ironmasters Richard Jesson and John Wright had been used there. In 1810 the Darbys built a pair of new blast furnaces at Dawley Castle.

The Coalbrookdale partnership's railways were transformed by the substitution of the L-shaped plate rails developed by John Curr of Sheffield which replaced the earlier pattern of iron edge rails. The Curr type of track, known in Shropshire as Jinney, Ginney or Jenny rails, was reckoned to be cheaper to lay and to operate than the earlier forms, and economies were anticipated when it was introduced. The plateway was nevertheless a cul-de-sac in railway technology, and its use in Shropshire after the mid-1790s, by all the ironmaking companies, was probably one reason why the stream of innovations in railway technology for which the area was famous for two centuries came to a stop. The developments between 1802 and 1830 which led directly to the modern main-line railway all took place in the North of England.

Chapter 6

DEPRESSION AND RECOVERY

BY 1810 THE HEIGHT of the war-time boom was past, and the iron trade was entering upon a period of falling prices. Difficulties became particularly severe after the Peace of 1815. Some of the Darbys' works were ill-placed to face increasing competition from ironworks in South Wales and the Black Country. The Coalbrookdale blast furnaces were finally blown out about 1818, and henceforth Coalbrookdale was simply a foundry, making castings from pig-iron smelted elsewhere. The Coalbrookdale forges continued in production until 1842-3. Thomas Butler, a Yorkshire ironmaster who visited Coalbrookdale in 1815, found 'all the machinery old and clumsy ... the works conducted upon the old plans of forty years ago'. He thought that the proprietors had made so much money during past periods of prosperity that they could afford to reduce production when prices were low. When Joshua Field visited Coalbrookdale in 1821 he found the 'Resolution' steam engine being dismantled, and the only castings being made at the foundry were parts for a sugar-mill for which the drawings were inadequate.

The Company continued to make bridges. In 1816 the parts for the footbridge over the Liffey at Dublin were cast at Coalbrookdale, to designs by John Windsor, one of the works foremen. The following year a 120-ft. cast-iron bridge crossing the Irwell between Salford and Strangeways was completed. In 1820 the Company provided the massive iron columns which support the arches of the Macclesfield Bridge which crosses the Regent's Canal to the north of Regent's Park in London.

Edmund Darby died in 1810 and was succeeded in the management of the ironworks by Francis Darby, son of Abraham Darby III, and Barnard Dickinson, husband of

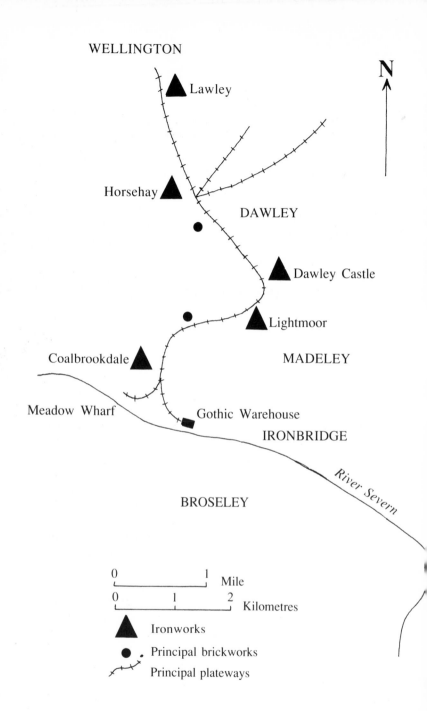

Fig. 3. Shropshire ironworks owned by the Darby family in the 19th century.

Plate 11. The Wellington or Halfpenny Bridge across the River Liffey in Dublin designed by John Windsor, and cast by the Coalbrookdale Company in 1816.

Francis's sister, Anne. Abraham Darby IV and Alfred Darby, sons of Edmund Darby, began to work for the Company in the late 1820s. In 1830 they assumed responsibility for the Horsehay works, where for two decades little had changed. The brothers began to institute ambitious reforms. One of the first was to remedy a source of waste which must have been evident for many years. The big steam engines at the ironworks drew their steam from boilers which were fired with high-quality coal, while the mine engines used slack which was of no value for any other purpose. The Darby brothers insisted that slack should also be used to fire the ironworks boilers, which not only reduced operating costs, saving between 600 and 700 tons of saleable coal a month, but prevented pit mounts from taking fire and filling the district with sulphur fumes. The furnace crews were kept upon constant alert by the constant presence of the Darby brothers. Waste products which had a high iron content were fed to the furnaces, considerably raising their output. When the brothers tried to motivate their furnacemen by introducing a bounty to be paid when production exceeded 60 tons a week per furnace, they suffered a set-back, since many loose castings, rails, wheels and tools were thrown surreptitiously into the furnaces. A new blast engine was built in

1834, and in 1838 the furnaces at Horsehay were converted to operate with J. B. Neilson's hot blast system.

Similar alterations were carried out at the forges. Joseph Hall's system of puddling, known as 'pig boiling', was introduced in 1832, although at first it was unpopular with the puddlers. Soon afterwards guide mills were installed. New steam engines were built to drive hammers and mills. At the furnaces, improvements were not carried out without arousing resentment. In 1837 there was a strike of underhands following attempts to improve the quality of the wrought-iron. Puddlers, understandably, resented being asked to produce good wrought-iron from what they claimed was inferior pig.

The foundry at Coalbrookdale was rationalised and the skilled labour force enlarged until, about 1851, it could reasonably be regarded as the largest foundry in the world. Architectural evidence suggests that there was a large-scale building programme during the 1850s or early 1860s. At Dawley Castle the furnaces were rebuilt, a new blowing-engine designed by Samuel Cookson of Coalbrookdale was installed, and hot blast was introduced in 1839. Also in 1839 the Company purchased the Lightmoor blast furnaces between Horsehay and Coal-

Plate 12. The Macclesfield Bridge across the Regent's Canal on the edge of Regent's Park in London. The bridge was built in 1820, the cast-iron columns being supplied by the Coalbrookdale Company, whose name is cast on the capitals.

Plate 13. Abraham Darby IV from a portrait in the Museum of Iron, Coalbrookdale.

brookdale, which dated from the 1750s. At a later date the Darbys acquired the Lawley furnace, formerly the property of the Ketley Company, which lay on the northern edge of the Darbys' mining territory.

The Darbys' five Shropshire ironworks were linked by plateways, and at some time after 1820 a new plateway route was constructed down the Lightmoor valley to Coalbrookdale, along which the products of Horsehay, Lightmoor, Dawley Castle and Lawley, together with coal and other minerals, could pass to the Dale works and the Severnside wharves. A warehouse in the Gothic style designed by Charles Crookes was built at the terminus of the plateway on Ludcroft Wharf. It now accommodates the Museum of the River. Abraham and Alfred Darby brought the operation of their plateways under direct company control, dispensing with the services of the contractors who had previously worked them.

From the mid-18th century the Darbys made bricks for their own use, but from the 1830s they extended this side of their activities. Brick kilns were built on several sites, and by 1855 the Company was selling building bricks, roofing tiles, crests and quarries from its wharf on the banks of the Severn. In the early 1860s the Darbys were exploiting beds of high-quality clays suitable for terracotta. In the 1862 International Exhibition the Coalbrookdale Company's display included ornamental terracotta vases and flower pots.

In the 1840s the Coalbrookdale Company ceased for a time to be a predominantly Shropshire concern. In 1844 Abraham Darby IV purchased the ironworks at Ebbw Vale in South Wales, and later bought other works in the region, at Abersychan, Abercarn and Pontypool. Subsequently William H.

and Charles Darby, sons of Richard Darby, obtained controlling interests in the Brymbo ironworks near Wrexham.

In many respects the Coalbrookdale Company lacked the zeal for innovation by which it had been distinguished in the 18th century. New ideas were tried hesitantly, and often some time after their success had been proved elsewhere, and innovations were often resisted by the workpeople. Nor was new technology always successful. In 1850 it was decided to close in the tops of the Horsehay furnaces, but the implementation of this decision was followed in 1851 and 1852 by two explosions, after which the tops were once more opened.

In 1839 the Coalbrookdale Company produced 800 tons of iron plates for the hull of Isambard Kingdom Brunel's *SS Great Britain*, which would certainly have been rolled at Horsehay. The Darbys had been connected with the shipping trade since the 1770s, when Abraham Darby III had interests in vessels sailing from Liverpool, and these were continued in the 1840s. In 1838 two wrought-iron plates measuring 10 ft. 7 in. by 5 ft. 1 in. were displayed in Liverpool. It was claimed that they were the largest ever rolled. Six years later the iron barque *Richard Cobden* was launched in Liverpool by Matilda Darby, wife of Abraham Darby IV. Correspondence in 1847 when the *SS Great Britain* ran aground in Ireland suggests that the Darbys had interests in the company which managed her.

Moulders at Coalbrookdale had long been able to produce highly-embellished architectural castings and ornamented items for domestic use, but in the late 1830s the Company began to manufacture art castings, busts, statues and bas-reliefs, some of them varnished or bronzed. An account written in 1855 suggests that the making of art castings, 'wedding the useful to the ornamental' began about 18 years before, that is in 1837. This branch of the foundry trade had originated at the Eisengiesserei ironworks outside the Oranienburg gate at Berlin, where, during the Napoleonic Wars, cast-iron copies were made of gold and silver valuables donated by Berliners to aid the Prussian war effort. A connection between Berlin and the products of Coalbrookdale is suggested by a comment in 1845 that 'the statues, figures and ornament worked in iron by the artists of Berlin have for some years enjoyed a European reputation', linked with the statement that the Coalbrookdale Company were 'the only British manufacturers who have as yet been their successful competitors'.

One of the first displays of art castings in England was at the National Anti-Corn Law League Bazaar at Covent Garden, London, in 1845. Most of the Darbys were enthusiastic Free Traders and gave generous support to the League. The Coalbrookdale Company display at the Bazaar included statues of J. W. von Goethe, Napoleon Bonaparte, the Duke of Welling-

Plate 14. The cast-iron statue of Oliver Cromwell, displayed by the Coalbrookdale Company at the International Exhibition of 1862. The statue along with the ornamental gates which the company had displayed at the Exhibition was purchased by Warrington Corporation. It now stands outside council offices in Warrington.

ton and Benjamin Franklin, firescreens decorated with images of Anti-Corn Law League heroes, five cast-iron tables, and a fountain incorporating a crocodile and a snake.

The Great Exhibition at the Crystal Palace in 1851 brought further fame to the Darbys as makers of art castings. At the entrance to the north transept of the Crystal Palace stood a set of ornamental gates, 60 ft. wide, cast at Coalbrookdale. Another contribution to the Exhibition was a towering cast-iron dome, 30 ft. high, sheltering a figure of an Eagle-Slayer with his bow. A slain eagle was pinned to the roof transfixed by an arrow. The company also exhibited an ornamental fountain, 'The Boy and the Swan', a statue of Andromeda exposed to a sea monster and a cast-iron altar-rail. John Bell, one of the most fashionable designers of the time, designed the Eagle-Slayer and Andromeda, but Charles Crookes, manager of the Coalbrookdale works, was responsible for the ornamental gates and the dome which sheltered the Eagle-Slayer. Andromeda was one of the successes of the Great Exhibition, and was described by one critic as 'altogether a design of exquisite beauty'. The pedestal, on which were cast small figures representing the Andromeda legend, was compared to the work of the Renaissance silversmith Benvenuto Cellini.

After the Exhibition closed, Andromeda was purchased for £300 by Queen Victoria and placed in the grounds of her house at Osborne in the Isle of Wight. In January 1852 the Commissioners for the Exhibition invited Abraham Darby IV to re-erect the ceremonial gates at the entrance to Kensington Gardens, not far from where, within a few years, the Albert Hall and the Albert Memorial were to be built. Charles Crookes supervised the re-erection of the gates. They still stand, although damage from motor traffic has necessitated many repairs.

The Coalbrookdale Company also contributed to the less successful international exhibition of 1862. Again there was a set of ornamental gates, this time more elaborate, with extravagantly florid classical capitals on the columns, which were surmounted by figures of angels. The writer of the exhibition catalogue remarked of the Company:

While it furnishes millions of dwellings with stoves and other household necessaries of a cheap kind, it adorns also the mansions and the palaces of the aristocracy ... while they fabricate huge machines that move vast ships and weighty carriages over land and sea, they give due consideration to the requirements of a refined life.

Exhibits included a hall table, a hall fireplace, with the fire overlooked from each side by a dog mounted on a cast-iron pedestal, two lamp pillars and a huge candelabrum. For gardens and conservatories there were vases, fountains and flowerpots. The most spectacular of the Coalbrookdale exhibits was a larger-than-life-size statue of Oliver Cromwell, based on a design by John Bell.

The Coalbrookdale Company also displayed art castings at international exhibitions in Dublin in 1853 and in Paris in 1855. At the Vienna exhibition of 1873 they gained the Medal of Progress, the highest award available, for a set of wrought-iron carriage gates in the medieval style, decorated with cast-iron panels, ornamented with oak, rose, apple and pomegranate leaves. Statues and fountains were sent to many parts of the world, one of the most distant destinations being Lyttleton near Canterbury, New Zealand, to which the Company despatched a cast-iron statue of the eminent colonial administrator, John Robert Godley, in 1866.

The traditional aspects of work at the Coalbrookdale foundry continued. Pots, pans, kettles and other forms of domestic hollowware continued to be cast, quantities of architectural ironwork were manufactured, and steam engines and bridges remained important products. In 1839 the Company supplied a 370-hp pumping-engine, with a 70-inch cylinder, for the Bog lead mines in south Shropshire. It was named the *Queen Victoria*. A large engine was also supplied to work the blowing machines at Abraham Darby IV's blast furnaces at Ebbw Vale. In 1824 and 1830 fine iron bridges were erected to the design of Joseph Potter, county surveyor for Staffordshire, at Alrewas and Mavesyn Ridware. In 1863-4 the Company built some small shunting locomotives, one of which can still be seen at Coalbrookdale.

Plate 15. One of the largest steam engines ever built by the
Coalbrookdale Company, constructed in the 1850s for blast furnaces in
Ebbw Vale, which were purchased by Abraham Darby IV and his
partners in 1844.

At the time of the 1851 census 13 members of the Darby
family were living in Coalbrookdale. Lucy, widow of Edmund
Darby, aged 69, lived in Dale House with her daughter, Mary.
Both were described as 'gentlewomen', and they employed four
resident house servants. Next door at Rosehill House lived
Richard Darby, then aged 63, who was described as a 'retired
Iron Master', although his two sons, William and Charles, were
apparently still active in the works, since they were called Iron
Masters. The best-known of the Darby houses, Sunniside, was
unoccupied, following the death of Francis Darby in 1850. Abraham Darby IV lived at the Chestnuts, and was described as a
'land and mine proprietor'. Darby and his wife employed six
resident servants: a lady's maid, a cook, two housemaids, a
butler and a footman. Finally, at the White House lived Hannah,
widow of Francis Darby, and her daughter Adelaide, with
Hannah's mother, and five resident servants.

From this time the connection of the Darby family with the
ironworks gradually diminished. Alfred Darby and Abraham

Darby IV reduced their commitments in managing the works in 1849. They were members of the fifth generation of Darbys to manage the Coalbrookdale ironworks, and by this time, as so many other families of successful industrialists had done at an earlier stage, they sought to settle on landed estates. During 1851 Abraham Darby IV and his wife went to live at Stoke Court, near Slough, following a dispute over Francis Darby's property. Alfred Darby leased Stanley Hall, the Jacobean mansion near Bridgnorth.

In 1876-9 Rebecca Darby, widow of Alfred Darby, who died in 1852, commissioned Richard Norman Shaw to build for her a new house at Adcote, north of Shrewsbury. Shaw was then one of the most celebrated architects in Britain, and Adcote is one of his most accomplished works. The house was sumptuously decorated with glass by William Morris and ceramics by William de Morgan.

The activities of the Coalbrookdale Company contracted in the latter part of the 19th century. In the early 1860s the blast furnaces at Horsehay ceased operation. The Company stopped smelting iron in 1883 when the furnaces at Dawley Castle and Lightmoor were blown out. Almost all the blast furnaces in Shropshire ceased to work at this period, the high costs of raw materials making it almost impossible for them to compete with ironworks nearer to the coast, which were able to make use of cheap, imported ores. The Horsehay forges were offered for sale in 1886, and were taken over by the Simpson family, who developed Horsehay as a bridge-building concern which continued until the 1980s. By 1900 the Coalbrookdale Company's principal concerns were its brickworks and the foundry at Coalbrookdale itself, which had been retained in spite of threats of closure, and still employed over 1,000 men. Abraham Darby IV died in 1878. He had been living at Treberfydd, Llangasty-tallyllyn, in South Wales but was interred in the Quaker burial ground at Coalbrookdale. Obituaries acknowledged his eminence in the South Wales iron trade.

From the 1850s, the day-to-day direction of the Shropshire ironworks of the Coalbrookdale Company was left in the hands of managers - Charles Crookes, from 1850 to 1866, and William Gregory Norris, from 1866 to 1897. In 1881 the Coalbrookdale

Company Limited was recognised as a public limited liability company, and from 1886 until 1925 Alfred Darby II served as its chairman. His retirement brought to an end the direct links between the Darbys and the ironworks, although since the late 1960s members of the family have been active in the Ironbridge Gorge Museum Trust.

Chapter 7

HOMES AND FAMILIES

FIVE GENERATIONS of the Darby family lived in Coalbrookdale and were involved with the management of the ironworks. From the time the children of Abraham Darby II were of
age there were often several Darby households in the dale and,
naturally enough, many houses are associated with the family.
Indeed, all the mansions on the western side of Coalbrookdale
have probably, at some time or other, been occupied by Darbys.
Abraham Darby I lived at White End near the Upper Forge,
which is now demolished, and then at Madeley Court. He was
building the house in Coalbrookdale, now called Dale House, at
the time of his death. Abraham Darby II spent the early years of
his married life there, but he built a new house on top of the hill
to the west in about 1750. This stood among ornamental
grounds, and was named Sunniside. It was demolished in 1856.
North of Sunniside lay the White House, which was itself re-
named Sunniside after the demolition of the original house of
that name. It was demolished in the 1950s. Dale House was
enlarged, probably in the 1770s. It is now being restored by the
Ironbridge Gorge Museum Trust. Rosehill House, sometimes
called The Grange, which dates from the 1730s, was occupied
by various managers of the works, and in the 19th century was
the home of Richard Darby. It has been restored by the Ironbridge Gorge Museum Trust as a 19th-century ironmaster's
residence. The Chestnuts, which also survives, is an early 19th-
century house, built for Sarah Darby, which was the home for
some years of Abraham Darby IV.

Like other ironmasters of the 18th century the Darbys were
often short of labour. They attracted workers to their mines,
furnaces and forges by offering them higher wages than could
be obtained in agricultural employment, and by providing

housing which was generally of a better standard than was usual in rural areas. While many of the iron-making and mining hamlets of the Shropshire Coalfield have now been swept away, the Darby settlements at Horsehay and Coalbrookdale remain as impressive monuments to the social history of the Industrial Revolution period.

Coalbrookdale retains the character of a small, highly-developed industrial community. The growth of the ironworks was gradual, the pattern of landholding complex, and the topography rugged, so that most of the houses are in small groups rather than long terraces. Tea Kettle Row, a terrace of six cottages which stands behind Rosehill House, was built by the Coalbrookdale Company in the 1740s and can be seen on engravings published in 1758. Carpenters' Row, a group of eight cottages and two wash-houses on the eastern side of the works, dates from the 1780s. Opposite Holy Trinity church is Church Row, or Charity Row, which was originally built for the widows of workmen.

Houses built by the Darbys for their workpeople can also be seen at Horsehay. The Old Row (now called Pool View) looks, over the pool where water to power the first furnaces was

Plate 16. The second house in Coalbrookdale to be named Sunniside, previously named the White House. It was demolished in the 1950s.

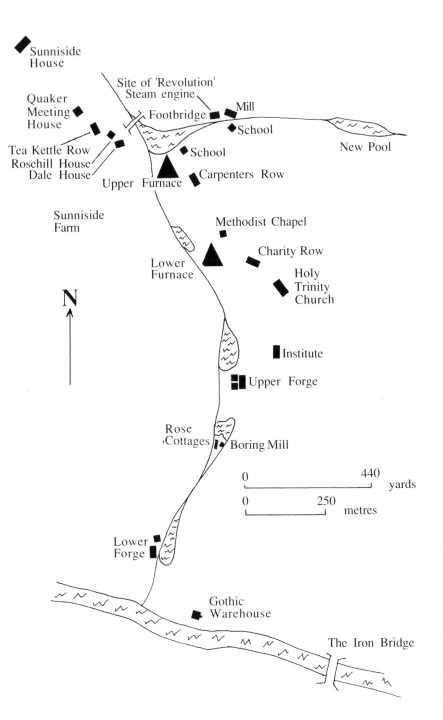

Fig. 4. Sketch map of Coalbrookdale.

Plate 17. Rosehill House (sometimes known as The Grange),
Coalbrookdale. Rosehill House was built in the 1730s, probably by
Richard Ford. In the 19th century it was the home for nearly 50 years of
Richard Darby, youngest son of Abraham Darby III. The house has been
restored by the Ironbridge Gorge Museum Trust.

impounded. The row was built in at least three phases, probably
quite soon after the works started in 1755. The houses, originally
consisting of four rooms each, were spacious for the period.
The New Row, further north, was built in the 1830s 'for the
better class of workmen', and the status of its occupants was

signified by such details as Gothic drip moulds and decorative ceramic devices over the doorways. Frame Lane Row, near Horsehay, is a surviving but much-altered example of rather plainer houses built by the company for brickmakers in the 1830s.

Not all the Darbys' workpeople lived in Coalbrookdale or Horsehay, or, indeed, in company housing of any sort. Census returns show that many must have walked daily to their work from the towns of Dawley and Madeley, and from squatter settlements like Holywell Lane in Little Dawley.

Coalbrookdale retains an impressive number of communal buildings. Abraham Darby III's accounts show that in 1786 he began to pay a yearly rent for a corn mill, and that he was re-building a mill, paying for masons' and millwrights' work, and for millstones and dressing cloths. This was probably the mill in Coalbrookdale which in 1801 was being worked by injection water from the *Resolution* steam engine. It was used at times by workmen for grinding their grain. The surviving mill building probably dates from the time when the *Resolution* was dismantled in the early 1820s. The buildings of two 19th-century schools, one for boys and one for girls, remain in Coalbrookdale. Pool Hill School, Dawley, was built by the Company to a design by Charles Crookes, in the same extravagant Gothic style which Crookes employed for the warehouse by the Severn which now accommodates the Museum of the River. The last of the Quaker meeting houses in Coalbrookdale was demolished *c*.1950, but the burial ground is preserved by the Ironbridge Gorge Museum Trust, as is that at Broseley, where Abraham Darby I was buried. In the 18th and 19th centuries the Wesleyan Methodists attracted followers in Coalbrookdale, initially as a result of the work of the saintly John Fletcher, vicar of Madeley from 1760 to 1785. Fletcher himself was responsible for building the first Methodist meeting house in Coalbrookdale, which was all but complete at the time of his death in 1785. Subsequently, during the period when his widow was the leader of the local Methodists, the Darbys from time to time visited Methodist services. The founding of the first Sunday Schools in the district in the early 1780s followed a suggestion made to John Fletcher by Abiah Darby.

The fourth Abraham Darby turned from his family's traditional Quakerism to the Church of England. In 1850 Anglican services commenced in the boys' school at Coalbrookdale. In December 1851 the foundation stone was laid of a new church dedicated to the Holy Trinity, the cost of which was borne by Abraham Darby IV. The workmen collected money for a peal of eight bells. The church, designed by the London architects Reeves and Voysey, was consecrated in 1854. The pew doors are of cast-iron and there are iron tombs in the graveyard.

Another notable addition to the life and landscape of Coalbrookdale in the mid-19th century was the Literary and Scientific Institution. The first moves towards the establishment of an institution were begun in 1852, and at a public meeting in January 1853 a formal resolution was adopted, proposing the founding of 'the Coalbrookdale Literary and Scientific Institution'. In 1856 a School of Art was founded in Coalbrookdale with the object of promoting high standards of design in the foundry. Accommodation for both these bodies was provided in a new building to the design of Charles Crookes, constructed by the Company in 1859, and consisting of a lecture hall, library, reading-room and art room, and a residence for a librarian. The style was described as Tudor Gothic, and the builders were proud that they had used the Coalbrookdale Company's blue and yellow bricks throughout. Among those present at the opening were Alfred Darby IV, the two M.P.s for the Borough of Wenlock, Dr. Matthew Webb, father of the channel swimmer, and Dr. Benjamin Kennedy, headmaster of Shrewsbury School.

In 1850 the place of the Darbys in local society was illustrated by the celebrations heralding the birth of a son to Alfred Darby and his wife, which resembled contemporary festivities on landed estates in Shropshire. A procession of nearly 4,000 employees, all wearing pink and white scarves, followed a route encompassing the whole of the district where the Darbys had mines and ironworks. It was headed by two men on horseback, Benjamin Poole, a dwarf, and the celebrated Horsehay giant, William Ball, who weighed over 40 stone and had to be lifted onto his horse by a specially-erected crane. At Horsehay a meal with 15,140 pounds of meat (19 bullocks and 42 sheep) was consumed, with 1,700 loaves and 1,000 gallons of ale. Brass bands played, and banners were displayed lauding the achievements of the Darbys. In the following week celebrations included a tea party for 1,000 children, a dinner for supervisory employees and a grand ball.

The Darbys played a prominent role in public affairs. Like many Victorian Quakers they supported the anti-slavery and teetotal movements, and were active in the Anti-Corn Law League. From the time of the Reform Bill agitation of the early 1830s they participated in the politics of the Borough of Wenlock in which Coalbrookdale was situated. Their support of Liberalism often brought them into conflict with local landed families.

The Darbys were not the only important ironmasters in Shropshire. None of them individually could match the powerful amalgam of piety and business acumen which characterised their partner, Richard Reynolds, nor the intellectual virtuosity and scientific zeal of William Reynolds, nor the drive and entrepreneurial skills of John Wilkinson. Nor were the Darbys the only iron-makers in Shropshire to provide good quality dwellings for their workpeople, and to show interest in their education and recreation. The Darbys were unique because over no less than five generations they made important contributions to the iron industry in Great Britain, and remained throughout this period active in the management of their works, and within the communities in which their workpeople lived.

Chapter 8

SURVIVALS

THE GREATEST CONCENTRATION of products of, and buildings associated with, the Darbys is, of course, in the Shropshire coalfield. At Coalbrookdale (SJ 667047) the Old Furnace, incorporating parts of that in which Abraham Darby I first smelted iron ore with coke in 1709, is protected by a modern cover building, and displayed as part of the Ironbridge Gorge Museum. Adjacent to the furnace, housed in the Great Warehouse built by the Darbys in the 1830s, is the Museum of Iron, opened in 1979, the best European museum concerned with the industry. It includes large collections of the products of Coalbrookdale. Nearby Rosehill House has been restored by the Ironbridge Gorge Museum Trust as a 19th-century ironmaster's residence, in which many objects which once belonged to the Darbys are displayed. Dale House is currently being restored by the Museum Trust. On the hill above Dale House and Rosehill is the Quaker Burial Ground in which Abraham Darby II, Abraham Darby III, Abraham Darby IV, Abiah Darby and William Reynolds, amongst others, are interred. Buildings in Coalbrookdale connected with the Darbys include the two former schools, the mill, now a private residence, three terraces of 18th-century workpeople's cottages, and the Coalbrookdale Institute, now a youth hostel.

Elsewhere in the Shropshire coalfield the only ironworks sites associated with the Darbys which now merit a visit are the Madeley Wood (or Bedlam) blast furnaces (SJ 680033), which are in the care of the Ironbridge Gorge Museum Trust, and Horsehay (SJ 673073) where the pool constructed for the ironworks in the 1750s is lined by two long terraces of workers' cottages. At the Blists Hill Open Air Museum (entrance at SJ 696036) there are few exhibits directly connected with the

Plate 18. The study at Rosehill House, as restored by the Ironbridge Gorge Museum Trust. The 18th-century desk is thought to have belonged to Abraham Darby III.

Darbys, but the site includes the Hay Inclined Plane and a restored section of the Shropshire Canal, for which Samuel Darby was treasurer. At Blists Hill it is possible to see demonstrations of two processes with which the Darbys were closely linked, the production of iron castings, and the manufacture of wrought-iron by puddling. A collection of Caughley porcelain which belonged to Alfred Darby II is displayed in the Coalport China Museum (SJ 696024). Madeley Court (SJ 695052), one-time residence of Abraham Darby I, and the Hay Farm, Madeley (SJ 697030), for a time the home of Abraham Darby III, have both been restored as hotels.

The most notable of the Darby monuments, the Iron Bridge (SJ 627033) was restored between 1973 and 1980. There is an information centre in the tollhouse at its southern end. Several other cast-iron bridges made by the Darbys remain in use. The Albert Edward Bridge (SJ 661037) at Coalbrookdale, cast at Horsehay in the early 1860s, carries the railway to the Iron-bridge power station. In Worcestershire the 'twin' of this bridge, the Royal Victoria Bridge, carries the restored Severn Valley Railway over the Severn near Arley (SO 766793). The Cound Arbour bridge near Shrewsbury (SJ 555053) which bears the inscription 'Cast at Coalbrookdale 1797' is still open to traffic, and an attractive Coalbrookdale bridge of 1828 carries the

Plate 19. The dining room at Rosehill House, as restored by the Ironbridge Gorge Museum Trust. The set of Chippendale chairs dates from 1777, and the dinner service was made for Alfred Darby and Rebecca Christie on their marriage in 1848. The portrait is of Francis Darby.

Plate 20. The Old Furnace, Coalbrookdale, while it was being uncovered by Allied Ironfounders Ltd. under the direction of Dr. G. F. Williams in 1959.

Severn towpath over the mouth of the Borle Brook near Highley (SO 753817). The present steel truss bridge over the Severn at Buildwas (SJ 654044) incorporates the stone abutments, cast-iron base plates and an inscription from Telford's bridge of 1795-6. In Staffordshire there are Coalbrookdale bridges of 1824 at Alrewas (SK 188139) and of 1830 at Mavesyn Ridware (SK 092167), and in Bath two Coalbrookdale bridges of 1800 cross the Kennet and Avon Canal in Sydney Gardens (ST 758653). In London the inscription 'Coalbrookdale' can be seen on the cast-iron piers of the Macclesfield Bridge over the Regent's Canal on the north side of Regent's Park, and in Dublin it is still possible to cross the Liffey on the footbridge cast at Coalbrookdale in 1816.

In public places throughout the West Midlands and further afield it is possible to find cast-iron garden furniture, statues, fountains, ornamental railings, church safes, pumps and heating stoves made at Coalbrookdale. In private homes, antique shops and museums are numerous cast-iron statuettes, relief medallions, smoothing irons and cake plates. In London the much-repaired gates from the Great Exhibition of 1851 stand at the entrance to Kensington Gardens near the Albert Memorial. In Warrington the gates from the 1862 exhibition stand outside the town hall, not far from the statue of Oliver Cromwell, cast at Coalbrookdale for the same exhibition. Castings of John Bell's statue of the Eagle-Slayer are displayed in the Museum of Iron at Coalbrookdale, and outside the Bethnal Green Museum. The model of the Iron Bridge presented by Abraham Darby III to the Society of Arts in 1787 is displayed in the bridges gallery of the Science Museum, London. Many of the wrought-iron plates of the SS *Great Britain*, now on display in Bristol, are doubtless those rolled at Horsehay in the 1830s, and in the National Railway Museum, York, is a section of cast-iron pipe made at Coalbrookdale for the atmospheric system on the London and Croydon Railway in the 1840s.

FURTHER READING

The place of the Darbys in their regional setting is examined in
Barrie Trinder, *The Industrial Revolution in Shropshire* (Second
edition, Phillimore, 1981), which is fully referenced and contains
an extensive bibliography. Arthur Raistrick, *Dynasty of
Ironfounders* (1953), most recently reprinted by Sessions of York
in 1989, is a more detailed study of the Darby and Reynolds
families. The same author's *Quakers in Science and Industry*
(1953 and reprints) shows the Darbys in their national Quaker
context. Nancy Cox's article, 'Imagination and Innovation of an
Industrial Pioneer: the First Abraham Darby', in *Industrial
Archaeology Review*, XII.2, 1990, has transformed our
understanding of the career of Abraham Darby I. For
Abraham Darby I's part in the brass industry, see also Joan
Day, *Bristol Brass* (David and Charles, Newton Abbot, 1973).
Rachel Labouchere, *Abiah Darby 1716-1793 of Coalbrookdale:
Wife of Abraham Darby II* (Sessions, York, 1988) is a valuable
study of the most influential of the Darby women. Neil Cossons
and Barrie Trinder, *The Iron Bridge* (Moonraker, Bradford-on-
Avon, 1979) is a detailed study of the most celebrated structure
associated with the Darbys. Stuart Smith's *A View from the Iron
Bridge* (Thames and Hudson, London, 1979) is the definitive
review of the impact made by the landscape of the Ironbridge
Gorge upon painters and other artists. W. Grant Muter, *The
Buildings of an Industrial Community: Coalbrookdale and
Ironbridge* (Phillimore, 1979) is a detailed study of the
architecture. A much fuller treatment of the architecture and
archaeology of the Gorge appears in the reports of the Nuffield
Survey of the Gorge by Catherine Clark and Judith Alfrey (Ironbridge Institute 1986-). Barrie Trinder, *The Most Extraordinary
District in the World: Ironbridge and Coalbrookdale* (Second
edition, Phillimore, 1988) is an anthology of writers' impressions

of the district from the 1740s to the 1950s. Research on the Darby's role in the production of art castings is contained in Ian Lawley, 'Art and Ornament in Iron: Design and the Coalbrookdale Company', in *Design and Industry* (The Design Council, London, 1980). A detailed analysis of local society between 1660 and 1750 is to be found in Barrie Trinder and Jeff Cox, *Yeomen and Colliers in Telford: the probate inventories of Dawley, Lilleshall, Wellington and Wrockwardine* (Phillimore, 1980). The most recent survey of the broader aspects of the history of the Shropshire coalfield is volume XI of the *Victoria History of Shropshire* (Oxford University Press, 1985). Barrie Trinder, *A Description of Coalbrookdale in 1801* (Ironbridge Gorge Museum Trust, 1970 and reprints) is an annotated edition of a manuscript account written by a local resident. Ken Jones, Maurice Hunt, John Malam and Barrie Trinder, 'Holywell Lane: A Squatter Community in the Shropshire Coalfield', in *Industrial Archaeology Review*, VI.3, 1982, is a detailed history of a community in which lived many employees of the Coalbrookdale Company.

The latest general survey of the history of the iron industry is J. R. Harris, *The British Iron Industry 1700-1850,* which provides a guide to some of the more recent specialist literature. For an understanding of the technology of the iron industry, W. K. V. Gale, *Iron and Steel* (Longmans, London, 1969) can be recommended. M. J. T. Lewis, *Early Wooden Railways* (Routledge and Kegan Paul, London, 1970) remains the standard work on the evolution of railway technology, and discusses fully the development of the Shropshire railway. Charles Hadfield, *Canals of the West Midlands* (David and Charles, Newton Abbot, 1966) is the standard work on waterways.

INDEX

Adcote, Shropshire, 57
Adderley, Shropshire, 44
Air furnaces, 10
Anti-Corn Law League, 53, 54, 65
Arkwright, Sir Richard, 23
Armaments, 17
Art castings, 52, 53, 54, 55, 69
Attingham Park, Shropshire, 12, 44
Ball, William, 64
Banks, Joseph, 27
Bath, 42, 69
Bell, John, 55, 64, 70
Benthall, Shropshire, 10, 31, 32, 33, 39
Birmingham, 3, 15, 16
Bishton, John, 41
Black Country, 3, 4, 7
Blakeway, Edward, 32
Blast furnaces, workings of, 5
Blists Hill, 67, 68
Bloomery furnaces, 8
Boilers, 46
Boulton, Matthew, 28, 39
Brass trade, 3, 4, 9, 11, 12, 13
Brickworks, 7, 31, 51
Bridgnorth, Shropshire, 20, 27, 31, 43
Bristol, 3, 4, 9, 10, 11, 13, 15, 25, 38
Brooke, Sir Basil, 8
Broseley, Shropshire, 4, 13, 14, 20, 22, 31, 32, 39, 63
Brymbo ironworks, 52
Buildwas, Shropshire, 31, 36, 69
Canals, 37, 38, 39, 67

Chainmaking, 1, 38
Champion, Nehemiah, 15
Charcoal, use in ironmaking, 6, 7
Chestnuts, The, 59
Church of England, 64
Clee Hills, 6, 12
Coal mines, 7, 20, 24, 25, 28, 31
Coalbrookdale, Shropshire, 1, 4, 7, 8, 60, 63, 66
Coalbrookdale Company, 41, 42, 43, 45, 51
Coalbrookdale Institute, 64, 67
Coalbrookdale ironworks:
  before 1708, 7, 8, 18;
  managers and partners, 8, 9;
  trade and products, 15, 16, 18, 44, 45;
  forges, 12, 18, 27, 28;
  foundry and furnaces, 9, 10, 11, 13, 15, 16, 17, 18, 19, 27, 28, 35, 41, 44, 45, 46, 47, 50, 52, 54, 55, 57, 66
Coalport, Shropshire, 32, 38, 41, 68
Coke, use in ironmaking, 9, 10, 13, 18, 21, 23, 28
Coniston, Cumbria, 11
Copper works, 11, 13
Cort, Henry, 27, 39, 45, 46
Cound bridges, 43, 68
Cranage, George and Thomas, 27
Cromwell, Oliver, 70
Crookes, Charles, 51, 54, 57, 63
Crystal Palace. See Great Exhibition
Curr, John, 39, 46

Dale'House, 12, 67
Darby:
 Abiah, 18, 19, 22, 23, 26, 63, 67
 Abraham I (d.1717), 3, 4, 9, 10,
  11, 12, 13, 14, 15, 23, 26, 59,
  68;
 Abraham II (d.1763), 15, 17,
  18, 19, 20, 21, 22, 23, 24, 25,
  26, 27, 42, 59;
 Abraham III (d.1789), 25, 26,
  27, 28, 30, 31, 32, 33, 34, 35,
  36, 37, 38, 39, 40, 41, 47, 52,
  62, 63, 67, 68, 70;
 Abraham IV (d.1878), 26, 49,
  51, 55, 56, 57, 59, 64, 67;
 Adelaide, 56;
 Alfred I (d.1852), 26, 49, 51,
  57, 64, 67;
 Alfred II (d.1925), 58;
 Anne, 49;
 Charles, 46, 52, 56;
 Deborah, 26, 42;
 Edmund, 26, 37, 41, 42, 44, 47,
  49, 56;
 Esther, 3;
 Francis, 26, 41, 47, 56;
 Hannah, 25, 26, 56;
 John I (d.1700), 3;
 John II (d. 1725), 3, 26;
 Lucy, 56;
 Mary (née Sergeant), 26;
 Mary, 26, 27, 56;
 Matilda, 52;
 Rebecca (née Smith), 26;
 Rebecca, 42, 57;
 Richard, 26, 52, 56, 62;
 Samuel, 26, 32, 35, 36, 37, 38,
  41, 42, 67;
 Sarah, 59;
 William, 26, 51, 52, 56
Darwin, Erasmus, 40
Dawley, Shropshire, 20, 37, 45,
 46, 50, 51, 57, 63
Dearman, Richard, 42
Dickinson, Barnard, 47
Ditton Priors, Shropshire, 45

Donnington Wood, Shropshire, 25,
 27, 37
Donnington Wood ironworks, 28,
 41
Dublin, 47, 55, 69
Dudley, 'Dud', 7
Dundonald, Archibald Cochrane,
 9th Earl of, 28, 39
Ebbw Vale ironworks, 51, 55, 56
Edge family, 1
Farming, 30, 31
Fineries, 5, 6
Fletcher, Rev. John, 63
Fletcher, Mary, 63
Flint, John, 38
Foley family, 21
Ford, Richard, 15, 17, 18, 19, 23,
 62
Forest of Dean, 4, 6, 7
Forges, 5, 6
Fox, Meshack, 9
Fox, Shadrach, 9
Frame Lane, Shropshire, 63
Freeth, Jonathan, 3
Fry, Joseph, 38
Gainsborough, Lincs., 16
Gilbert, John and Thomas, 37
Gilpin, Mark, 42
Goldney, Thomas I, 15, 17
Goldney, Thomas II, 17, 19, 20, 25
Gower, 2nd Earl (and 1st
 Marquess of Stafford), 20, 25,
 28, 37
Grange, The. See Rosehill House
Great Britain, 52, 70
Great Exhibition, 54, 70
Gregory, Thomas, 35
Hartshorne, Richard, 10, 13, 16, 17
Hay Farm, 30, 31, 68
Haycock, John Hiram, 35
Holywell Lane, Shropshire, 63
Horsehay, Shropshire, 20, 23, 60,
 63, 64, 67
Horsehay ironworks, 20, 21, 22,
 23, 24, 25, 27, 28, 41, 45, 46,
 49, 50, 51, 52, 57, 68

Horton, Robert, 38
Housing, 60, 62, 63
Inclined planes, 38
International exhibitions, 54, 55, 70
Iron and ironmaking:
    organisation of, 4-7, 19, 20, 24;
    methods, 4-7, 8;
    cast iron, 5;
    pig iron, 5;
    wrought iron, 4, 5, 8, 12, 27
Iron Bridge, The, 1, 31, 32, 33, 34, 35, 36, 39, 40, 42, 43, 55, 68
Iron bridges, 42, 43
Ironbridge Gorge Museum Trust, 58, 59, 63, 66, 67
Jesson, Richard, 45, 46
Jessop, William, 39
Kemberton ironworks, 7, 12, 13
Ketley ironworks, 20, 22, 25, 27, 28, 38, 39, 41, 51
Knight family, 21
Lawley ironworks, 51
Leighton, Shropshire, 7, 12, 36
Lichfield, Staffs., 31
Lightmoor ironworks, 22, 50, 51, 57
Lilleshall Company, 41
Limestone, 5, 10, 20, 30, 32, 37
Liverpool, 27, 30, 52
Locomotives, 43, 55
Luccock family, 1, 10
McAdam, John Loudon, 39
Macclesfield Bridge (London), 47
Madeley, Shropshire, 8, 13, 30, 31, 32, 36, 37, 41, 63
Madeley Court, 14, 68
Madeley Wood ironworks, 22, 28, 41, 67
Malt and malting, 3, 9
Malt mills, 3
Manchester, 15
Methodists, 63
Mills, 20, 31, 44, 63, 67
Much Wenlock, Shropshire, 10, 36
Myddle, Shropshire, 11

Napoleonic Wars, 45, 46, 47, 52
Nash, John, 42, 43, 44
National Railway Museum, 70
Netherlands, The, 42
Newdale, Shropshire, 22, 39
Newcomen, Thomas, 16, 18, 44
Norris, William Gregory, 57
Paris, 55
Parrot, Stannier, 16
Poole, Benjamin, 64
Port Books, 10
Potter, Joseph, 55
Pritchard, Thomas Farnolls, 32, 33
Puddling, 27, 39, 45, 46, 50, 67
Quakers, 1, 3, 4, 13, 14, 15, 17, 22, 24, 25, 38, 39, 57, 63, 64, 65, 67
Railways, 16, 17, 19, 20, 23, 24, 25, 27, 30, 46, 51, 68, 70
Rathbone:
    Hannah (née Reynolds), 26, 27;
    Joseph, 26, 27, 28, 35;
    Mary (née Darby), 27;
    William, 26, 27
Reynolds:
    Hannah, 26, 27;
    Hannah (née Darby), 25, 26;
    Rebecca (née Gulson), 25, 26;
    Richard, 25, 26, 35, 39, 41, 65;
    William, 2, 25, 26, 27, 28, 35, 38, 39, 40, 65, 67
Richard Cobden, 52
Riots, 31
Road transport, 16, 30, 31, 36, 37, 39
Rooker, Michael Angelo, 35
Rosehill House, 59, 60, 62, 67, 68
Salford, 47, 63, 64, 67
Schools, 63
Science, 40
Science Museum, London, 35
Sergeant, Joshua, 15
Seven Years War, 22
Severn Navigation, 7, 10, 24, 32, 37, 69
Shaw, Richard Norman, 57

Shrewsbury, 15, 38, 40, 44
Simpson family, 57
Smythe, Sir Edward, 35
Society of Friends. *See* Quakers
Steam engines, 16, 18, 20, 23, 24,
    28, 30, 39, 43, 44, 46, 47, 49,
    50, 55, 56, 63
Steel, 4, 12
Sunniside, 56, 59
Sunniside Farm, 21, 30, 31
Tar ovens, 28, 39
Telford, Thomas, 39, 43, 69
Tern ironworks, 11, 12, 13
Terracotta, 51
Thomas, John, 10
Tontine Hotel, 35, 36
Trentham Park, Staffs., 42
Trevithick, Richard, 43, 44

Vienna, 55
Wages, 59
Warrington, Lancs., 70
Water power, 5, 6, 17, 18, 20, 23,
    28, 30
Watt, James, 28, 39, 43, 44
White End, 13, 59
White House, The, 59
Wilkinson, John, 22, 28, 32, 35, 39,
    65
Willey ironworks, 7, 22, 28, 32
Williams, William, 30, 35
Wood, Charles, 19
Wright, John, 45, 46
Wrockwardine Wood, Shropshire,
    25, 38
Young, George, 37